D1255874

THE GOLDEN PATH

The Golden Path

*Interviews with Disciples of
Sri Aurobindo and the Mother
of the Sri Aurobindo Ashram and Auroville*

Anie Nunnally

Published by

East West Cultural Center,
The Sri Aurobindo Center of
Los Angeles, California

First Edition 2004

Copyright © Anie Nunnally 2004

ISBN 0-930736-05-2

Published by
East West Cultural Center,
12329 Marshall Street,
Culver City, CA, 90230.

Printed at Sri Aurobindo Ashram Press
Pondicherry - 605 002.
Printed in India.

*This Book is offered
at the Lotus Feet of the
Divine Mother*

Acknowledgements

The author wishes to acknowledge and thank the following organizations and individuals that have given of their time, effort and financial support toward the creation of THE GOLDEN PATH.

To all the interviewees I extend my deepest gratitude.

To Sri Manoj Das Gupta and the Trustees of the Sri Aurobindo Ashram, Pondicherry, India, for permission to use texts and photographs.

The Foundation for World Education, USA,

The East West Cultural Center, USA; and

Debashish Banerji, Stuart Schoen, Donna Sharkey, Diana Arias and Dorian Schneidman.

Richard Hartz and Sue Crothers, Proof readers, Sri Aurobindo Ashram Archives; Kiran Kakad, Photographer, Sri Aurobindo Ashram Archives.

Santosh Krinsky, USA,

Sam Spanier and Eric Hughes of Matagiri, USA and Deirdre McGuire, USA.

Lynda Lester, Larry Seidlitz and Dave Hutchinson of COLLABORATION Journal, USA.

Foreword

While she was in the body, the Mother at the Sri Aurobindo Ashram in Pondicherry, India, was both externally and internally the heart and raison d'être of everyone's existence there and each one's daily life gravitated around her and her radiant presence. The sense of a collective yoga was intensely experienced and the "how-to's" were close at hand, because the Mother was available to answer to every specific circumstance. Anie Nunnally, whose name Anie was given to her by the Mother, spent four precious years at the Sri Aurobindo Ashram and Auroville from 1968 to 1972. She had gone there with the Mother's permission and with the sole purpose of being under her spiritual aegis. During her years there she was associated with the Mother through letters and both public and private darshans. This was the time during which the Mother was at the height of her intense inner work with the descent of the supramental consciousness. Anie became deeply aware of the Mother's yoga shakti in her own life and in the lives of sadhaks of the Ashram with whom she has formed many deep and abiding friendships.

When the Mother withdrew from the physical body in 1973, many felt that the Integral Yoga would become impracticable and that the Ashram would crumble since there was now no external guidance. A similar mood had arisen like a cloud after Sri Aurobindo's passing in 1950, but the Mother's presence and action were quick to dispel this mood. She more than amply filled in the space left by Sri Aurobindo's departure, and for good reason, for had he not said "The Mother's Consciousness and mine are the same"? But now there was no successor. How could the yoga be done? How would the Ashram run? From where would the answers come?

For those who had the concrete experience of the working of Sri Aurobindo's and the Mother's yogic force in their lives, this was no issue. Exclusively reliant on the inner guidance, nothing had changed. If anything, Their action had grown more available, more universal. Both in the Ashram and in Auroville the Mother had left a solid core of such sadhaks whose unshakeable practice of yoga grounded Sri Aurobindo's and the Mother's living consciousness not only in their own lives but in the larger collective context. Individuals and the collective continued to grow horizontally and vertically — more lives were touched, the yoga progressed. The grand experiment of Sri Aurobindo and the Mother, preparing human lives to embody a divine life on earth, proceeded on schedule, paving the golden path to supermanhood.

Can the same be asserted for the present? In this rapidly changing world, with its trappings of modernity impacting every facet of life (and the Ashram and Auroville are in no way exempt from this), with the physical memories of Sri Aurobindo and the Mother growing more remote by the day and the generations of early sadhaks progressively dwindling, once more the doubtful question raises its anxious head — does the yoga have a future?

Surprisingly, today the yoga is alive and well, not only at the Ashram and Auroville, but throughout the world. Increasing numbers are making the Ashram environs their home, the Ashram life their lives. It is the same for Auroville and testimony for the proliferation of the sadhana in all walks of life all over the world is borne by the swelling populations that arrive each year at the Ashram for darshans. Among these, the majority have never had any contact with either Sri Aurobindo or the Mother in Their physical embodiment and yet most feel Them intimately guiding their lives. A book, a photo or the example of a disciple has touched their lives and a door has opened — they have been invited to the Great Adventure; a guiding hand has reached out to them from across the gulf that separates us from the unknowable mystery and has taken them by the hand.

But in spite of this, except for the few, our steps, bereft of the external guidance, have been at best faltering and we have turned for pointers to the lives and teachings of the Masters. What was it like to live in the physical presence of the greatest open secret and mystery of our times — the incarnated presence among human beings of the divine consciousness in double form? What effect did it have on the inner life? What living trace did it leave behind that the dwindling core of direct disciples continues to bear testimony to in their lives? There are the writings, letters and conversations of Sri Aurobindo and the Mother and a great deal has been written by disciples in the form of reminiscences, all of which are invaluable help to seekers of the Integral Yoga today.

But what Anie has sought to capture in this collection of interviews is the golden thread of the yoga — the growing psychic flame of inner lives lived in the proximity of Sri Aurobindo and the Mother. Bringing her own deep commit-

ment to the yoga and her reverence for the avatars, she helps
unravel the same in her interviews — twelve very different
forms of inner growth and expression, united only by their
articulate recognition of having been and continuing to be
shaped, moulded by Sri Aurobindo and the Mother. Anie's
subjects range from those advanced in age (one of whom has
since left the body) who have lived in nearness to Sri
Aurobindo to those who, middle aged now, have grown up
as children under the tender loving care of the Mother. Remarkable also is the number and quality of the female voices
— those sensibilities which have otherwise grappled with
circumstances and had their mystic transactions with the invisible in silence behind closed walls but brought here to
expression through the feminine sympathy of the interviewer.
Each one of these personalities has responded to the divine
guidance with an integral eagerness that has made well-
formed multi-faceted jewels of them and living torches of
the evolutionary force, creative in the most essential sense of
the term.

Their sharing opens up for us multiple windows into the
continuing and unfailing yogic action of Sri Aurobindo and
the Mother and brings us into contact with this action. Con-
templating these words, we find ourselves vicarious members of the select inner circle, led from within, kindled as by
contagion. We are no longer alone trying to work out the
obstinate difficulties of the nature, the impossible intricacies
of new consciousness formations within. We are carried on
the wave of relationship, the Guru and the Mother surround
our lives with the sweetness of Their infinite love, calling us
to Their embrace. We forget the way of personal effort and

learn the way of surrender; instead of our own progress our minds become full of Their remembrance. Like the lives voicing themselves so unreservedly here, we discover the sunlit path, the wisdom of divine childhood. We find ourselves immersed in Them and learn the secret that to dwell on Them is to let Them dwell in us — to make us Theirs, to make us one with Them in the one and only way that each of us can so be. This is the golden path of the Integral Yoga and as we open this book, it is a door to this path that opens itself in our hearts.

DEBASHISH BANERJI
President, East-West Cultural Center
The Sri Aurobindo Center of Los Angeles, California

Author's Commentary

As time progresses there will be many more spiritual aspirants who are called to the yoga of Sri Aurobindo and the Mother. They will never have received Their personal darshan.

Those privileged beings who have actually seen Sri Aurobindo and the Mother and who have received darshan of these two great yogis and dual avatars are becoming fewer in number with each passing year.

For this reason I was inspired during a 1999 visit to Pondicherry to interview two such Ashram elders, Sri Amal Kiran and Sri Udar Pinto, the latter of whom has since passed on. Upon returning to the U.S., after my 1999 visit, their two interviews were published in the American journal *Collaboration* and in the East-West Cultural Center's online journal called *Jyoti*. The response from readers was so positive that I returned to India in 2000 and 2002 to complete ten more interviews with a grant made possible to me by the Foundation for World Education. The idea for a book of these interviews developed during the course of my visits to the Ashram and Auroville.

During my four years of residence in Pondicherry and Auroville I had always been deeply touched by the inner light that radiated from those beautiful souls who had come there to practice the Integral Yoga. They had left their countries of origin and other parts of India to live there and to surrender their former lives to the spiritual life of the Ashram. In this book, I wanted to tell their stories. I wanted *The Golden Path* to serve as an exalting and inspirational experience as it shares the inner revelations of these twelve disciples who have lived in the Ashram or Auroville for many years and whose lives were dramatically changed by their meetings with Sri Aurobindo and the Mother.

In this regard I feel that the book takes on something of a biblical perspective. How many through the centuries could have come to revere Jesus Christ to such an extent without his advent having been chronicled by his disciples?

The interviews could have continued, for there are many more worthy individuals, but I stopped at twelve and have chosen a diversified group of six men and six women from Indian, European and American backgrounds.

The account by these extraordinary people of their personal experiences, their meetings with Sri Aurobindo and the Mother and their practice of the Integral Yoga, under the guidance of Sri Aurobindo and the Mother, is enlightening and uplifting. During my time with them I felt Their palpable and powerful presence and received my own personal darshan.

It is my hope for everyone who reads *The Golden Path* that they, also, will experience some aspect of a personal darshan.

ANIE NUNNALLY
Los Angeles, California
December 2003

CONTENTS

Foreword

Author's Commentary

Two Nonagenarians ... 3

Amal Kiran ... 7

Udar Pinto ... 27

Gauri Pinto ... 47

Tehmi Masalawalla ... 67

Sunanda Poddar ... 87

Richard Pearson ... 119

Jhumur Bhattacharya ... 141

Anurakta ... 159

Anu Purani ... 177

Aster Patel ... 193

Krishna Tewari ... 221

Amrit (Howard) Iriyama ... 235

To walk through life armoured against all fear, peril and disaster, only two things are needed, two that go always together — the Grace of the Divine Mother and on your side an inner state made up of faith, sincerity and surrender. Let your faith be pure, candid and perfect. An egoistic faith in the mental and vital being tainted by ambition, pride, vanity, mental arrogance, vital self-will, personal demand, desire for the petty satisfactions of the lower nature is a low and smoke-obscured flame that cannot burn upwards to heaven.

Sri Aurobindo, *The Mother*

THE MOTHER

SRI AUROBINDO

I saw the Omnipotent's flaming pioneers
Over the heavenly verge which turns towards life
Come crowding down the amber stairs of birth;
Forerunners of a divine multitude,
Out of the paths of the morning star they came
Into the little room of mortal life.
I saw them cross the twilight of an age,
The sun-eyed children of a marvellous dawn,
The great creators with wide brows of calm,
The massive barrier-breakers of the world
And wrestlers with destiny in her lists of will,
The labourers in the quarries of the gods,
The messengers of the Incommunicable,
The architects of immortality.
Into the fallen human sphere they came,
Faces that wore the Immortal's glory still,
Voices that communed still with the thoughts of God,
Bodies made beautiful by the spirit's light,
Carrying the magic word, the mystic fire,
Carrying the Dionysian cup of joy,
Approaching eyes of a diviner man,
Lips chanting an unknown anthem of the soul,
Feet echoing in the corridors of Time.
High priests of wisdom, sweetness, might and bliss,
Discoverers of beauty's sunlit ways
And swimmers of Love's laughing fiery floods
And dancers within rapture's golden doors,
Their tread one day shall change the suffering earth
And justify the light on Nature's face.

(Sri Aurobindo, *Savitri*, Book III, Canto IV, pp. 343-344)

Amal

Udar

Two Nonagenarians

On a visit to the Ashram in December of 1999 I interviewed two long-time members; Sri K.D. Sethna (named Amal-Kiran by Sri Aurobindo meaning "a clear ray") and Sri Udar Pinto, (in Sanskrit Udar means "generous") who were 95 and 93 years young respectively at that time. These two nonagenarians graciously shared with me the illuminating experiences of their darshans and early days in the Ashram with Sri Aurobindo and the Mother. It is difficult to imagine what it would be like to stand in the presence of Sri Aurobindo, to encounter the infinite in a physical form and to even correspond with Him directly. Both these men had that privilege and I am greatly honored to tell their stories.

Both gentlemen had broken their hips in 1999 and were confined to wheel chairs, but neither showed any signs of broken spirits nor were they lacking in a healthy sense of humor. (Amal referred to himself as being "legi-capped" rather than "handicapped" as he was also stricken with polio in his early childhood). However, at this stage in life he says of himself "I have a fire in my heart which age cannot quench"....

Years of sadhana and dedication to higher pursuits have been kind to the minds and bodies of these two extraordinary beings. Their lovely, radiant, wrinkle-free skin, vibrant, sparkling, intelligent eyes and mental clarity are often not found in men of a much younger age. Amal-da, as he is affectionately called in the ashram, is a writer of poetry of exceptional merit (*The Secret Splendour: Collected Poems*) as well as a critic of poetry and author of numerous books on scientific thought and history. He was a correspondent with Sri Aurobindo on *Savitri* while Sri Aurobindo was writing this monumental tome. He was also founder and for half a century, editor of *Mother India: A Monthly Review of Culture*. Even now he remains in contact with legions of the scholarly and those in literary circles from all around the world.

Udar Pinto came to Sri Aurobindo and the Mother as a businessman living in Pondicherry. He founded the Harpagon Atelier, makers of furniture and stainless steel products and was a personal secretary to the Mother, seeing Her on a daily basis and taking care of correspondence and numerous business matters on Her behalf. He continued to recuperate at home and to receive visitors almost daily until his passing on December 7, 2001 at age 95. For many years, at 5PM each day, he read aloud from Sri Aurobindo's epic poem, Savitri, to a group of rapt listeners who gathered for these recitations and meditations that followed in his sitting room at his home called "Fenêtres".

We have all met in previous lives otherwise we would not have come together in this life. We are one family and have worked through the ages for the victory of the Divine and its manifestation on earth.

The Mother

Amal Kiran

Amal Kiran

Amal now calls home the Ashram Nursing Home on Goubert Avenue where he has resided since May 1999 after his hip was broken. He does not want to return to his house as he is well taken care of at the nursing facility and is freed from all the responsibilities of "housekeeping", as he says. The monsoon rains were teeming on many days that I visited him, but there was always sunshine when I entered his room because of his warm, welcoming and sunny disposition. This was true, also, of his lovely assistant, Minna Paladino. He is given daily physical therapy sessions, receives many visitors and when I arrived he was often sitting in the sun room overlooking the Bay of Bengal, pondering the tireless waves and surf that pound the concrete walls along the boulevard. He seemed quite peaceful and contented.

Amal was born Kekushru (Kekoo) D. Sethna on November 25, 1904 in Bombay. The family were members of the Parsi community in Bombay; descendants of the Zoroastrian Persians who fled their homeland to India in the 7th and 8th centuries to escape Muslim persecution. His father was a prominent doctor in Bombay and the family adhered to the traditional Zoroastrian faith. Young Kekoo passed through a phase of religious fervor in his childhood and prayed daily from the Zoroastrian Book of Prayers called Avesta, in the ancient Persian language of Avestan. When he was afflicted with polio at the age of around 2 years, his father took him to London for surgery to correct the paralysis. The surgery was somewhat successful but a slight limp remained. This, how-ever, obviously did not stand in the way of his many lifetime achievements. I asked him what were some of his childhood ambitions and he said that at one point in his youth he wanted to be just like Sherlock Holmes because he "admired his mys-terious and probing mind, his quick intelligence and high brow". He used to ask the barber to cut his hair so that he would look just like Sherlock Holmes!

Soon young Kekoo was writing verse and novelettes and binding the books himself. As he grew into his teen years he began to doubt the existence of God and began to probe sci-entific literature. He was soon reading Joseph McCabe, an exponent of the German Haeckel's Science of Materialism. His father was incensed about this and told Kekoo that Haeckel was an atheist and that he did not want the "wrath of the Almighty brought down upon his house." The young boy replied, "the wrath will come if the Almighty comes!" His father said, "I will call upon all the learned of the community to come and reason with you." The son replied, "I look for-ward to talking to them." (The great thinker was being "hatched".) Amal said that he never would have dreamt that after his father's death (which came not long after this pe-riod) he would eventually take up the spiritual life at the Sri Aurobindo Ashram. (He became a brilliant student of litera-ture and philosophy at St. Xavier's College in Bombay and was studying for his MA when he arrived at the Ashram in 1927. He gave up all formal education after joining the Ashram.)

The interest in the science of materialism with its theories and debates regarding free will vs. predestination, continued for a time but would soon change. A new way of thinking was on the horizon. His girlfriend, at that time, spoke to him of a Bengali yogi and devotee of Sri Krishna who visited Bombay periodically. His name was Pagal ("mad for Krishna") Harnath. They went to see him. Amal put a question. "I believe that the universe is ruled by fixed laws. Where, then, does God come in?" The yogi replied, "If there are laws then there must be a lawgiver"! Amal thought he was being verbally tricked but sensed something in his tone that led him to believe that it was an answer beyond the intellect. This was the first time that his intellectual interrogation was squelched. A sense of something deeper was expressing itself, something of intuitive knowledge, so he could not bring himself to engage in mental questioning. This event led him to begin reading Vivekananda and Sri Ramakrishna. In this period he went to another yogi, Yogi Devji, who taught him some breathing exercises. The yogi went about the room touching people on the top of the head and Amal felt a powerful electrical current down his spine. He had people render themselves immobile and draw the whole of their being upward from the feet through the top of the head where he said there would be "spiritual presences in the room ready to help them". Amal tried to do this and suddenly found himself in an out-of-body experience in quite a conscious way. He knew he wasn't dreaming. He was watching himself do this extraordinary thing; then he asked a self-conscious question, "How is this possible?" With this question there was a sudden rush back into the body. He said that with this he learned not by any argument, but by actual experience that we are more than just a body. This, finally, was the proof for him

that he wasn't just a physical form and no materialist thinking could convince him otherwise. From this point onwards
his entire outlook on reality changed.

How He Came to Sri Aurobindo

One day he went to the Crawford Market in Bombay to buy
a pair of shoes. Upon his return home he took notice of the
newspaper in which the shoes were wrapped. He opened up
the paper and there before him was an article entitled "A
Visit with Aurobindo Ghose". He avidly read the article and
said, "this is the kind of yoga I'd like to do...under a master
yogi like Sri Aurobindo who can read in six different lan-
guages and appear in more than one place at a time!" He did
not think it odd that a yogi could appear in more than one
place at a time, but a yogi who could master so many lan-
guages, including Greek and Latin, was a remarkable phenomenon to him. He wrote to the Ashram and received a
reply from Sri A.B. Purani saying that he and his girlfriend
could come there and "try it out". Before leaving, he satisfied his grandfather, now the family patriarch, and married
his Parsi girlfriend. This was a good decision as, tradition-
ally, newly married couples in India receive sizeable sums
of money from family and friends, so now he had sufficient
funds to travel to Pondicherry. This was 1927 and he was
twenty-three years old. After some time in Pondicherry he
sent a telegram to his grandfather that read "Enjoying pic-
turesque Pondicherry"! After they had been there for nine
months his grandfather wrote back "Where is the baby?"
The reply was that they had had a new inner birth and that

was the "baby"! He and his wife Lalita, who had accepted
Sri Aurobindo and the Mother, eventually lived separately
and she stayed on in the Ashram for almost 10 years before
returning to Bombay. Amal Kiran ("A clear ray") was given
his name by Sri Aurobindo in 1930. Amal's poetic genius
was recognized and nurtured under the guidance and inspiration of Sri Aurobindo and he ultimately entered into correspondence with Sri Aurobindo on *Savitri*. After Lalita left,
Sri Aurobindo warned Amal against any serious affairs with
women. However, there was a young Parsi woman in Bombay, Sehra, who had loved him years before and had never
married. When he returned to Bombay on a visit they were
reunited and married. He told her he would give her ten
years of married life and then he would return to Pondicherry. *Mother India* was launched in 1949 and he continued to edit the magazine from Bombay. He and Sehra
eventually returned to the Ashram on February 12, 1954 and
Sehra passed away on April 24, 1980.

Following are some of the questions I put to Amal and his
answers:

> *Would you describe your first darshan with Sri
> Aurobindo and the Mother? What experiences did you
> have with them?*

The first darshan with the Mother I had the impression of a
radiance all around her. When I first saw Sri Aurobindo I
had the sense of something leonine, as well as a mountain-
ous calm. He leaned forward and blessed me with both

hands about my head. The Mother kept smiling all the time as if to set me at ease in the presence of Sri Aurobindo. My turn to go to them was to follow an American couple that I overheard discussing whom to bow to first. They solved the problem by bowing between them. This way they touched the feet of neither but had the rare experience of being blessed by both of them at the same time. I looked at Sri Aurobindo and saw him gently moving his head forward and backward with an expression on his face as if he saw my inmost being. I felt afterwards a little disappointed with myself for having examined his look and general appearance. I liked the shape of his nose and the way he seemed to look deep within me. But afterwards, I did feel disappointed with myself for having concentrated on his outer appearance. When I met the Mother later on I asked her, "Mother, has Sri Aurobindo said anything about me?" She said, "Yes, he told me that this young man has a good face." So it seemed to be "tit for tat". I was a little disappointed but I told myself that to have a good face in Sri Aurobindo's eyes cannot but mean a great deal — at least it meant that I could face the difficulties of the yogic life. Sri Aurobindo had a soft, very soft voice, I am told, but I never heard him speak.

> *Can you describe the atmosphere of the Ashram when Mother and Sri Aurobindo were in their physical bodies and the difference since that time?*

The general atmosphere of the Ashram did not change radically. When both Sri Aurobindo and the Mother had left their bodies, I could still feel their presence. Perhaps because their subtle physical was said to have extended a number of miles beyond their bodies. I remember being told that their subtle physical auras extended up to the Lake Estate, several miles away. So it may be said that they hold us close to them even at a great distance.

> *In what way did your sadhana change after they left their bodies? How has the sadhana changed for you at this stage in life and what new forms has it taken?*

The sadhana has not fundamentally changed since my first experience which was the opening of the heart center about six months or so after I settled in Pondicherry. I was persistently wanting this opening of the heart and several times I made the Mother touch me with her hand in the middle of my chest asking her to break me open there and at last there was an opening. At that time, I realized just how shut human beings are in their heart region. With that opening came the sense not only of a great wideness but also of a lovely atmosphere full of flowers and fragrances accompanying this happy warmth. Sometimes the sense of the opening was so intense that I felt almost breathless and prayed that this heavenly feeling would never go away.

> *What changes do you see taking place in the Ashram in the future and will it be different, in any way, from what it is now?*

So long as a nucleus of sadhaks exists in the Ashram who

are really doing the yoga, the Ashram will remain as it always has been.

> *What do you see as being the strongest attributes and contributions of Americans to the work of Mother and Sri Aurobindo?*

Mother felt that external help for the growth of the Ashram would come imminently from America, but she said there would be a sort of tantalizing connection. I remember her saying that Ganesh, the Lord of Wealth, would always help her but often in a wayward way. There were times when the Ashram was almost desperately in need of money. The Mother had to sell her own saris to obtain the needed relief. There were some American followers who bought the saris and then offered them back to the Mother. A great deal of money began to pour in to the Ashram from America after the Mother's departure.

I always felt a special admiration for those who had never seen Mother or Sri Aurobindo in their physical bodies and yet could dedicate themselves to the Ashram life...especially those people from America and other countries. I know of some who had come here as fulfilling a part of their pilgrimage in India but having been here for some time dropped their idea of seeking elsewhere and stayed on in the Ashram. The first Americans to settle here were a couple named Mr. and Mrs. McPheeters. The husband went out to travel to various places and when he returned was not quite the same person. During his absence his wife became part of the small group that used to meet the Mother in the prosperity store

room before the soup ceremony took place. Janet McPheeters
would have stayed on if it had not been for her husband who
wished to return to America.

> *One difficulty occurring in the sadhana is straying from
> the path, doing what one knows not to do, becoming
> discouraged, etc. Did this happen in your sadhana?
> How to guard against this happening and what to do if
> and when it comes?*

Straying from the path and doing what one knows not to do
are real obstacles in yoga. Becoming discouraged now and
again is a very common phase but one can get over this condition by appealing again and again to the Divine for help.
In any kind of difficulty the most powerful help lies in praying to the Divine to carry one safely through the dark periods. The Divine is always ready to pick you up whenever
you fall. A certain passage in the Mother's *Prayers and
Meditations* has been the chief support of my yoga. It begins, "O Divine and adorable Mother, what is there that cannot be overcome with Thy Help?" There is also the passage,
"Thou hast promised to lead us all to our supreme destiny."
Not always to go on struggling but to appeal to the Mother
to take up our struggle is one of the major secrets of success. Perhaps it is best summed up in the formula "Remember and Offer". To practice this most fruitfully one must
stand back inwardly from the invading impressions.

> *Now that you are in your nineties, what has yoga done
> for you at this stage in your life?*

My paramount aspiration, as stated earlier, was to have the opening in the heart — what Sri Aurobindo called the Psychic Being. This gave me an intense feeling of joy that was self-existent. I was always afraid it would not last, but last it did, though not always at the same pitch. Ever since this first breakthrough there has always been a sense of a radiant response to the presence of the Mother and Sri Aurobindo.

Could you explain what it was like to be Sri Aurobindo's correspondent for Savitri?

A friend of mine with some literary accomplishment gave, on my invitation, his comments on *Savitri*. Mostly they were critical. I submitted them to Sri Aurobindo and he considered them by answering. He found them not sufficiently penetrating because the writer had no spiritual background, but as they were from an accomplished literary consciousness, Sri Aurobindo thought it worthwhile to enter into a discussion with him. When I sent a copy of Sri Aurobindo's answer to my friend he was rather apologetic and said that if he had known that Sri Aurobindo would read them, he would have been less "downright" in his tone. It was good that he was "downright" because thereby he gave Sri Aurobindo an opportunity to reply at length. Sri Aurobindo considered his comments as representative of a competent critical mind and he wanted this kind of mind to realize the newness of such poetry as *Savitri*, which was written from a yogic consciousness. Sri Aurobindo's answers to various criticisms by me helped to make clear the level from which Sri Aurobindo wrote his spiritual poetry. Sri Aurobindo said

my questions to him were based on some understanding of
the kind of poetry he wrote and the plane from which He
did so. Whereas, my friend's comments were lacking in
sympathetic understanding. *Savitri* struck me as opening up
an entirely new world not only of experiences but of literary expression. It was a great help to me because I was ea-
ger to write from what Sri Aurobindo called the overhead
planes. Of course I aspired to participate in that consciousness but more directly my aim was to open myself to the
influence and receive the direct utterance of poetry. It was
possible to be receptive to it without myself getting stationed on those higher levels. Sri Aurobindo distinguished
these levels as higher mind, illumined mind, intuitive mind
and overmind intuition. He considered these planes as being communicated by us through our poems. The sheer
overmind was difficult to tap and examples of the sheer
communication could be found mostly in the Rig Veda,
Upanishads and part of the Gita. It was interesting to realize that by silencing one's mind and keeping the consciousness looking upward, as it were, it was possible to write the
highest spiritual poetry now and again without being stationed on those overhead levels. It is also interesting to note
that one or two skillful changes in a poetic statement could
mean a leap from the mental level to the overhead one. A
striking example can be given by the small change made in
one line like:

"A cry to clasp in all the one God-hush"

A sheer uplifting of the plane can come by transferring

two words from the middle of the line to its end so that the
line would read:

"A cry to clasp the one God-hush in all"

The first version suggests that this cry could be suggested
by an effort to catch it while the other version transmits the
plane directly.

> *For many years you had been going to the samadhi for*
> *long meditations on a daily basis. Would you describe*
> *what you experienced in these meditations?*

There was a response from the samadhi towards me and
from myself towards the samadhi. The presence of Mother
and Sri Aurobindo became more intense during these visits
to the samadhi. Afterwards the persistent feeling was that I
carried the samadhi within myself, so I do not feel an acute
need to be physically face to face with it any longer.

*   *   *

Some days later I returned to the nursing home to visit Amal.
It was Christmas Eve morning and he was dressed in a bright
red shirt and was also wearing his ever-present bright and
happy smile. On this day, the last interview day, I had no
specific questions. We spoke of many things among them
being that of feeling the Mother's presence within. I told
him that after my near death experience from an automobile
accident in 1962, that the Mother had come to me miracu-

lously bringing me back from the portals of death. At that time she entered my consciousness, opened my psychic being, and since that time has remained permanently in my heart center. I stated that I felt Sri Aurobindo as a vast Presence looking down on me from very high above as the Purusha consciousness. Amal said "Yes, Sri Aurobindo is too large to live within our hearts; we live within him!"

Amal told me that the Mother said if someone came to her even once she did two things: she linked their outer being to their psychic being and the other was that she put out an emanation of herself to go with that person for all of their lifetime. That emanation would go out in accordance with the spiritual needs of the sadhak.

We discussed death further and he said that he spoke to the Mother on a crucial point about going on doing yoga life after life. The Mother said, "Death is not a part of our program!" Amal said he was thunder-struck by this statement. How then did Sri Aurobindo pass away? His passing was called "The Great Sacrifice". It was not a death in the ordinary sense. Paradoxically, Amal said, with his death the "power of death" died. Death as a regular, fixed principle of evolution no longer exists. Of course people still "die" but overcoming death and decay was the last victory of the work of Sri Aurobindo and the Mother for the earth and it is from the subtle physical plane that this work continues until it is completed.* Amal said that the Mother and Sri Aurobindo

*In the complete fulfillment of Sri Aurobindo's vision, physical immortality is seen as a culminating result and there was a belief in the early years of the Ashram that Sri Aurobindo, the Mother and all the (then few) disciples would become immortal. The Mother's later conversations (as in

have a "home", an actual "abode", on the subtle physical plane. Many ashramites have "visited" this plane and have seen them there.

After this discussion silence fell and we remained in this vast moment of eternity for quite some time. I quietly left with no further words exchanged.

Once more I visited this shining soul before leaving to return to the U.S. The meetings with Amal set in motion a deepening for me of my innermost being and my own personal sadhana. I came away with the feeling of intense joy and gratitude for having been graced to know of his experiences with the Mother and Sri Aurobindo, which brought me ever closer to them in this very personal and intimate sharing.

---

the *Agenda*), make clear that she was pushing the limits of her physical consciousness towards the immortal supramental body, but was unsure if it was to be done now. In this conversation with Amal Kiran, some time after Sri Aurobindo's passing, she affirms the view of a physical supramenta-lization in this life. Corresponding to this, she contextualizes Sri Aurobindo's passing as "The Great Sacrifice", which destroyed the "principle of death", so that physical death was no longer "necessary" and would eventually disappear, once the human physical consciousness awoke to this fact and eradicated the "habit". The "death" of the Mother herself, then, may also be seen in this light as a concession to the present human condition.

From *The Secret Splendour: Collected Poems of K.D. Sethna (Amal Kiran)*, pp. 70-71, 77-78.

This Errant Life

This errant life is dear although it dies;
And human lips are sweet though they but sing
Of stars estranged from us; and youth's emprise
Is wondrous yet, although an unsure thing.
Sky-lucent Bliss untouched by earthiness!
I fear to soar lest tender bonds decrease.
If Thou desirest my weak self to outgrow
Its mortal longings, lean down from above,
Temper the unborn light no thought can trace,
Suffuse my mood with a familiar glow.
For 'tis with mouth of clay I supplicate:
Speak to me heart to heart words intimate,
And all Thy formless glory turn to love
And mould Thy love into a human face.

SRI AUROBINDO'S COMMENTS:

"A very beautiful poem, one of the very best you have written. The last six lines, one may say even the last eight, are absolutely perfect. If you could always write like that, you would take your place among English poets and no low place either. I consider they can rank — these eight lines — with the very best in English poetry."

Ne Plus Ultra

(To a poet lost in sentimentalism)

A madrigal to enchant her — and no more?
With the brief beauty of her face — drunk, blind
To the inexhaustible vastnesses that lure
    The song-impetuous mind?
Is the keen voice of tuneful ecstasy
To be denied its winged omnipotence,
Its ancient kinship to immensity
    And dazzling suns?
When mystic grandeurs urge him from behind,
When all creation is a rapturous wind
Driving him towards an ever-limitless goal,
Can such pale moments crown the poet's soul?

Shall he — born nomad of the infinite heart!
Time-tamer! star-struck debauchee of light!
Warrior who hurls his spirit like a dart
    Across the terrible night
Of death to conquer immortality!—
Content with little loves that seek to bind
His giant feet with perishing joys, shall he
    Remain confined
To languors of a narrow paradise—
He in the mirroring depths of whose far eyes
The gods behold, overawed, the unnamable One
Beyond all gods, the Luminous, the Unknown?

SRI AUROBINDO'S COMMENT:

"This is magnificent. The three passages I have marked [lines 6 through 17] reach a high-water mark of poetic force, but the rest also is very fine. This poem can very well take its place by the other early poem [*This Errant Life*] which I sent you back the other day, though the tone is different — that other was more subtly perfect, this reaches another kind of summit through sustained height and grandeur."

Harin and Amal

Amal and Minna – Ashram Nursing Home Dec. 1999

*Go within your little person and
you will find the key which
opens all the doors.*

The Mother

Udar Pinto

Udar Pinto

No. 5 Rue St. Gilles is on the street in the French Quarter of Pondicherry directly behind the main compound of the Sri Aurobindo Ashram. "Golconde Guest House" is just a block down the street from this large French Colonial-style structure that the Mother had named "Fenêtres" (Windows). This is home to Udar Pinto, his English wife Mona, manager extraordinaire of Golconde, and their daughter Gauri, a teacher at the Sri Aurobindo International Centre of Education. Sri Aurobindo gave Udar (Generous) and Gauri (another name for Durga meaning the Fair One) their names but asked that Mona keep her own name as it reminded him of the Mona Lisa. At "Fenêtres" one enters into a glorious courtyard ablaze with vibrant colors of bougainvillea, marigolds, roses, other types of flowering plants, graceful arrangements of potted plants and an upstairs terrace filled with orchids. Gauri's animals (she rescues cats and dogs from the streets of Pondicherry and nurses them back to health) either playfully greet one at the door or in the case of some dogs stand back and snarl and growl suspiciously until one's purpose in visiting is cleared to their canine satisfaction.

Upstairs Udar has his quarters with a large vestibule where one can sit and wait for him. He then greets guests in his expansive sitting room with his faithful servant nearby. His bedroom is off to the side. I shall always remember these rooms as my first public darshan of the Mother was viewed

from that very space since Udar's quarters look out onto the
balcony adjoining Mother's rooms. That darshan was February 21, 1968; some thirty-two years ago! Udar had broken
his hip in 1999 and was recuperating at home after being in
the Ashram nursing facility for some time. When I entered
the room he was seated in a very large, high wheelchair; very
high above my own chair. He appeared so stately and in com-
mand that this gave me the impression of sitting before a
ruling monarch of empyrean stature. In fact he told me that
when the Ashram school staged "Perseus the Deliverer", one
of Sri Aurobindo's plays, he had played the role of King
Cepheus. One day he went to the Mother in his costume.
When she saw him she said, "Udar, I know where I have
seen you before, you were at one time a Roman emperor!"

Udar told me that he was born in Hubli in Karnataka (near
Goa) in April of 1907. His father was a businessman there
and did many things for the town of Hubli. The road they
lived on was called Pinto Road. His father had originally come
from Goa. Goa was colonized by the Portuguese and long
back Udar's family had taken on the Portuguese name of Pinto
and had completely lost all contact with their original Indian
name. He studied at the Good School in Goa and was brought
up in the Catholic Church. He said he was a good Catholic
and took his religion seriously as a young man. Later he began to find some rather foolish things in all religions which
is what ultimately led him to Sri Aurobindo. He passed his
exams in Hubli and was sent to Mussoorie in the mountains
of north India for further study. He wanted to take a degree
in engineering and was being prepared for that goal. However, by that time he had become rather unruly and was thrown

out of school. This was to be a turning point in his life. He stated that if he had remained there he would have graduated, gotten a good job and settled down to a "humdrum" life. After he was thrown out he attended another school in Belgaum and from there went on to Bombay to the Royal Institute of Science for a degree in engineering. He was then sent to England in 1929 where he spent four years and earned a degree in Aeronautical Engineering from the London University. However, there was nothing for him to do. There were no airplanes in India at that time so he had to go into business. He settled down in Pondicherry in 1935 because it had a reputation for being a good place to do business. He tried it out for two years and it proved to be prosperous. All of his friends were connected with the Ashram but at that time he was not interested nor did he ever visit the Ashram. He was a young man and a bon vivant. His friends came to his home for sumptuous dinners and whisky and sodas and "all kinds of things", he said. They would go back and tell the Mother stories of their visits to Pinto's house. She would say, "That Pinto fellow is spoiling my children and I will catch him one day." "Finally, she did," Udar said.

Udar had met his beloved Mona while attending school in England and she waited three years for him while he got settled in Pondicherry. Finally, in 1937, he sent for her and they were married. Their daughter, Gauri, was born at the end of that year in November.

First Darshan of Sri Aurobindo and the Mother

After Mona and Udar were married somebody suggested

that they should have darshan of Sri Aurobindo and the Mother so Udar arranged for this. "There were very few people in the Ashram in those days so there was no long queue," Udar said. In August of 1937 they had their first darshan. This is how Udar described that moment: "When I saw Sri Aurobindo for the first time I got a shock. I had seen kings and emperors in Europe, England and Asia whose clothes were majestic but the person inside quite ordinary. Here was a man wearing only a dhoti and chaddar (shawl) sitting bare-chested and looking like a king. I said to myself, 'at last I have seen royalty and majesty'. After that darshan we were very much drawn to the Ashram."

The War

The war began and Sri Aurobindo and the Mother took a keen interest in it. "All wars", said Sri Aurobindo, "are begun by the asura." The Second World War was an effort by the asura to destroy the work of Sri Aurobindo and the Mother for the earth's evolution toward the Supramental Light. Sri Aurobindo began to work occultly behind the scenes for the war effort even finding an opening to his Force in Sir Winston Churchill. Udar said there were very few radio sets in Pondicherry at that time and no radio broadcasting. Udar owned a radio set with sophisticated aerials and other equipment so he was able to tune into the BBC in order to receive news of the war. Pavitra (the Frenchman whose European name was P.B. Saint-Hilaire) and Pavita (an Englishwoman) used to come to Udar's house every night at 9:30 to take down the news in shorthand and

type and prepare it to send to Sri Aurobindo the same night.
Udar offered the radio set to the Mother but she refused it
by saying she had had "enough of ulcers"! Later on when
the war situation escalated they finally installed a
radio set in the Ashram.

Udar had begun to become more and more drawn to the
Ashram. By then the Government of India had started a Civil
Aviation Department and they knew of his degree in Aeronautical Engineering so they asked him to come and work
for them. He did not want to go as he and his family were
quite happy in the Ashram. Sri Aurobindo, however, told him
that he *must* do it. He wanted his children to work for the war
effort. Sri Aurobindo told him this was not a war between the
nations and people but a war between the Divine Forces and
the forces of the asura. Udar took his family out of Pondicherry and worked for the government successfully for one
year and was happy in New Delhi and so was Mona. Little
Gauri, however, at three years of age very much missed the
Mother. After one year he took a brief leave and brought
them back to Pondicherry. Sri Aurobindo then told him that
he had done enough and that he could return to the Ashram
to stay. He went back to New Delhi, gave a month's notice
and returned to the Ashram where he has lived since.

Golconde and Harpagon

The Nizam of Hyderabad through his Dewan, Sir Akbar
Hyderi, had given a sum of money to the Mother as she, at
one time, had spoken to him of wanting to build a residen-
tial building on some property the Ashram owned. Since the

money for the building had come from Hyderabad the Mother decided to give it a name associated with that state. She named it "Golconde", the French form of Golconda, after the famous fort and diamond mines in Hyderabad.

Antonin Raymond, a well-known Czechoslovakian architect and friend of Pavitra, came to the Ashram for a visit and eventually took on the project. Working with him on the Golconde project were the Japanese-American architect, George Nakashima and another Czechoslovakian architect by the name of Francicheck Sammer.

The building work had already begun by 1937 when Mona and Udar joined the Ashram but they were both associated with it from that time. The Mother put Mona in charge of Golconde before it was finished and gave her a room in which to work to prepare the linen and train the young Ashram ladies who were to work with her. She taught them to speak English as well. The Mother also gave Udar a small shed for his work. She called it Harpagon, which is the name of the miser in Molière's play *L'Avare* (The Miser). She said that the land had belonged to a very wealthy man and he could have given the land freely but instead he doubled the price! At first the Mother said "No", but then she decided to buy the land and name it after the miser. Ironically Udar's name means "generosity". There was so much work to be done. Large amounts of money were needed for the completion of the Golconde structure. There were things to be manufactured; some brass fittings were needed and machines were needed for manufacturing these parts to precision. Udar had no money as he had given all his money to the Mother. He needed at least two lakhs (200, 000 rupees) and asked the

The Golconde Guest House

View of Mother's Balcony
from Pinto Residence, Dec. 1999

Mother for this amount. The Mother gave him one rupee to start! At first he thought she was making a joke but then he realized that if she had given him the two lakhs it would be the two lakhs that would have actually done the work. He said, "by giving only one rupee it was therefore I who had to do it." He took up the challenge and worked very hard and happily and slowly until the job was done. Of course today Golconde and Harpagon are cherished units in the Ashram. Golconde is one of the most beautiful and unique buildings in the world with its teak furniture, Japanese-style black stone floors, walls of crushed seashells, giant louvered shutters and of course its lovely monastic peacefulness. Udar went on to develop Harpagon's many industries including furniture making and stainless steel products.

> *Can you describe Sri Aurobindo's voice and any other impressions you remember of him?*

Sri Aurobindo's voice had a beautiful, well-modulated sound. If you did not see him you would think that you were listening to a Cambridge-educated Englishman speaking. Sri Aurobindo just sat there looking as though he were gazing out into eternity in his great lonely days of descent into mortal life in order to help humanity.

[Udar chose not to personalize other impressions of Sri Aurobindo but instead he quoted a passage from *Savitri*, Book III, The Book of the Divine Mother, Canto IV, The Vision and the Boon. Udar said Sri Aurobindo was writing about King Aswapati in that passage and speaks in the third person, but he is actually writing about himself.]

Can you describe what it was like when Sri Aurobindo left his body?

I was in his room next to him when he left his body. I was handling the oxygen tank and then he went into a coma. I knew all the medical aspects of what it was like to be in a coma. However, in the case of Sri Aurobindo, it was altogether a conscious coma. No ordinary person talks in a coma. At one point he asked in a firm and clear voice: "Nirod, what is the time?" Nirodbaran looked shocked, but replied, "Sir, it is one o'clock." Sri Aurobindo said "I see" in a clear voice and then returned into the coma. Champaklal was massaging his feet. His breathing became slower and slower and then there was the last breath which I recognized. Dr. Sanyal asked me to turn off the oxygen tank and I went back and stood in the back of the room. I was quite calm and interested to see all that was happening. The Mother had no look of sorrow on her face at all. Neither did I feel sorrow for I knew that Sri Aurobindo had left his body consciously. In *Savitri* the Book of Death is very short. When Sri Aurobindo was asked about this he said, "You cannot expect to write about something you have never consciously experienced." So he experienced death consciously and will return to complete the Book of Death. Dr. Sanyal said, "Mother, everyone is in shock except for Udar." The Mother put me in charge of everything. She looked at me and said, "Udar, take charge of everything and come to me for instructions" and then she left the room.

Mother gave me instructions for the coffin that was made of solid wood and lined with silk. Sri Aurobindo was still lying on his bed and there was the most marvellous, golden light emanating from his body and a scent like a celestial perfume. After that the Mother told me how deep to go into the Samadhi and how to design it. I built the Samadhi not as a hole in the ground but as a vault with thick concrete walls nine inches thick with cement floors and a cement roof. I went down eight feet and built a four-foot room with cement slabs. Over that the Mother instructed me to build another room also with walls, a floor and a roof. She told me to fill it with clean river sand and to put a large slab on the top. Thus was the Samadhi built. The Samadhi was built according to the same outward pattern as the flower bed that had existed there. The top consisted of a long rectangular pattern going from east to west and next to it was a square. The Samadhi on top has kept that same pattern for flower decorations. The longer rectangle below houses the two rooms where the bodies of Sri Aurobindo and the Mother are entombed. The Mother gave me a prayer to be carved in marble in English and French and placed on either side. It reads:

December 9, 1950

"To Thee who hast been the material envelope of our Master, to Thee our infinite gratitude. Before Thee who hast done so much for us, who hast worked, struggled, suffered, hoped, endured so much, before Thee who hast willed all, attempted all, prepared, achieved all for us, before Thee we bow down and implore that we may never forget, even for a moment, all we owe to Thee."

After the Mother left her body I opened up the top room. I took out the clean river sand that had been lying over Sri Aurobindo's tomb from 1950 to 1973 and kept it in barrels. I made packets from the sand and gave them to many people and it helped them in sickness and pain and in times of trouble.

> *What changes do you see taking place in the Ashram in the future and will it be different in any way from what it is now?*

There have to be changes. We live in a changing world. The changes in the Ashram since the Mother's passing have not always been as good as they could be. Many people have not worked closely with the Mother nor even seen her physically. So, in many cases, there is very little knowledge of the Mother's way. Many people try to do things in their own way, to do what they think best and not always necessarily in keeping with what would have been the Mother's way. I always speak about the Mother to everyone but many go on preferring their own way.

> *What can you tell us of the Auroville project?*

Auroville was built as a city for the Divine to give a message to the world. The Mother told me to inaugurate Auroville. The Mother called in representatives from all the nations of the world and assigned to me the job of Master of Ceremonies. The Charter was read out in English. I announced each nation and while two young people from each

nation placed soil from their country into the lotus urn there
was an interpreter reading the charter in the language of that
particular nation. It all went so beautifully and was never
rehearsed. The Mother said Auroville did not need to follow
the divine life of the Ashram. She said they were to concentrate on building a new city for the Divine in their own way.
So, the ways of Auroville are different from those of the
Ashram and Aurovilians are not expected to follow the
Ashram way of living.

> *What advice would you give to new spiritual aspirants
> that would help them in their development and help
> them to integrate their lives in the world with its focus
> on materialism and the vital life?*

The word "spiritual" is often used in a loose manner. Generally people take it to mean a higher mind and life in an el-
ementary way but not necessarily a "spiritual" way. Spiritual
means the way of the spirit and nothing else. Very few people know what their spirit is. They know they have a soul
but how it operates they do not know. It is only when one
becomes conscious of the soul through sincere yogic discipline that one can become a true servant and instrument of
the Divine.

> *It seems that fewer young people are drawn to the yoga
> in America in these times. What more can we do to
> inspire interest in Sri Aurobindo and the Mother in the
> youth of our culture?*

One must keep a door open for those who want to come, but we are not here to proselytize and get disciples. If they come it is by their own choice and what they do with it is up to themselves.

> *What do you see as the strongest attributes of Americans and their contributions to the yoga?*

The Americans who have come to the Ashram are highly evolved people and their presence is a gift to the Ashram. Many Americans in the Archives department are wonderful men and women and have progressed very much inwardly and have contributed in many ways to the work and are of great value to the Ashram. I have a very good feeling about the Americans in the Ashram.

> *What were some of your experiences and impressions of North America when you visited in 1972?*

In 1972 the Government of India asked the Mother to select two people to give talks on Sri Aurobindo in connection with his Birth Centenary year; one to go to the East and one to go to the West. Sisir Kumar Ghosh was chosen to go to Japan and other Eastern countries and the Mother chose me to go to the West. I asked the Mother, "Why me? I am not a speaker on philosophy."

Then Mother said, "I have chosen you, so you must go!" The Mother said she would speak through me and that I did not need to worry for at all times she would remain very close to me. This was so in every instance.

When I reached America they began to call me "Swami-ji". I looked to see if there was anyone else around! I told them, "I am not a Swami, I am just an ordinary person whom Mother has sent to speak on Sri Aurobindo." When I later returned to the Ashram the Mother said, "They called you Swami-ji there?" I replied, "Yes, Mother." The Mother said, "I knew everything that happened to you in America. I was with you all the time and I am glad you did not accept the title of Swami-ji. If for any reason you should ever fall into that trap, I will come and break your head!"

I had a wonderful trip to America. I found the people generous and warm. We were often treated as guests at restaurants, people helped us freely on the road when our van broke down and in private homes we were received with gracious hospitality.

While I was visiting America there was a three-day seminar at Cornell University — an inter-religious conference. Leaders of all the world religions were invited. My hosts tried to get me on the program but it was declined because the conference had been planned two years prior. However, they said I could come and participate in the discussions, so I agreed. Suddenly I received a call from them that the main speaker had fallen ill and could I come and replace him? I said "Yes". They asked me to send a speech but I wrote that I only spoke extemporaneously.

This was accepted and all throughout I felt Mother's Presence and Help and even saw her face before me. The Mother had told me before I left India, "You have only to call me and I will be with you at once, at every moment I will be with you."

Can you share some of the advice that the Mother gave to you for your own personal sadhana?

One day I asked Mother, "I have been doing the yoga for many years but I am not absolutely certain how to do the yoga of Sri Aurobindo. I read all the books and try to do the yoga but I am not certain how far I have progressed." I asked the Mother to help me. "You are doing it all wrong," she said. "But what shall I do?" She replied, "I will do the yoga for you." I was thrilled! "What do I have to do?" I said. "Give yourself over to me and I will do it for you." I asked, "How do I surrender?" She said to me, "Do you sincerely want to?" I answered "Yes, certainly, Mother." Then Mother asked, "When you get up in the morning what is the first thing you do?" "I brush my teeth and as a matter of course I am thinking of all kinds of things and not at all consciously," I replied. Mother said, "Try and think of me while you are brushing your teeth. Talk to me keeping fully conscious while you wash your face and brush your teeth. When you eat that is the time you must be very conscious of me. Feel that I am eating with you and talk to me and enjoy your food. Let all the parts of your being remain conscious of me. Eat every mouthful with me and you will find that things taste so much better when you enjoy the food with me. When you go to sleep that is the time when you should be very conscious of me. Let me put you to sleep and then the whole night you will have a conscious sleep. When you awaken and begin your day you will then begin it in a more conscious way."

Since that conversation I have sincerely tried to make this effort. It may not always be complete and whole but I make the effort to remain fully conscious of the Mother's Presence in all my actions and activities.

How is the sadhana different for you at this stage in your life; what new forms, if any, has it taken?

At this stage of my life I just want to be always conscious of the Mother's Presence in me. I am always calling her and she never refuses to come. If I ask her for anything she gives it to me if it is useful for my sadhana. If not, then I know it is not and accept that. I have no regrets about anything at all. I am very happy to have served the Mother consciously and I want to be like that up to the end. If there is an end! The Mother told me not to accept death as inevitable. She said, "Don't say you are not going to die, but don't say you have to die. When it comes face it in full confidence of my support but fight it! Do not accept death!"

* * *

Udar remained silent for a few moments and then began to chant Mother's mantra "Om Namo Bhagavate" and then "Om Anandamayi". I sat quietly with him for some time and then left him in the atmosphere of that still, quiet space.

A few days later I returned to see him. It was December 17th, the day before my birthday, and Udar had developed a bronchial condition. I felt he was too weak for the interview and I did not want to tire him. However, he called me in to present me with flowers and beautifully wrapped birthday gifts. Udar had been my liaison to the Mother, delivering my numerous chits and letters to her during my years in the Ashram and prior to the time that I went there to live for three and a half years. He had been privy to all my innermost questions and concerns that were put before the Mother. He advised and counseled and inspired me as well with his great strength, wisdom and positive outlook. What a fitting name...Udar...for he was truly generous with his time, help, work, friendship and most of all the largesse of his inner being and spirit. He was always wearing the ever-present red rose such as was given to him daily by the Mother and for years after her passing he continued to wear a red rose.

Udar was ill with bronchitis for most of the remainder of my stay in Pondicherry. I saw him one last time before my departure with a group of French visitors who had come to see him.

He was in good humor that day and had us laughing heartily. About losing his voice to bronchitis he said: "In my household it does not make much difference as the women do most of the talking anyway!" He said, "Did you know that generally speaking, women are generally speaking?"

After all the time that I spent with Amal Kiran and Udar Pinto I reflected on these two souls who, with their very diverse backgrounds — one a scholar and writer and the other an engineer and businessman — had come to the Mother and Sri Aurobindo as young men and in a common bond had devoted their lives to the service of the Divine and to the Yoga of the Supramental. At this stage in their lives both have focussed their priorities on remaining open to the

Divine Light of the Mother and Sri Aurobindo for as long as they are in their present bodies. I could not have been more deeply touched nor blest to have dwelt for those days in the midst of their inspiring presence.

The essential character of Supermind is a Truth-Consciousness which knows by its own inherent right of nature, by its own light: it has not to arrive at knowledge but possesses it. It may indeed, especially in its evolutionary action, keep knowledge behind its apparent consciousness and bring it forward as if from behind the veil; but even then this veil is only an appearance and does not really exist: the knowledge was always there, the consciousness its possessor and present revealer.

Sri Aurobindo

Gauri Pinto

Gauri Pinto

(Teacher in the Sri Aurobindo International Centre of Education)

My return visit to "Fenêtres" on Rue St. Gilles in Pondicherry, home of the Pinto family, found me again being greeted at the door by the furry likes of "Starry", "Jackie-Boy", "Cutie", "Tina", "Brownie", "Radha" and others of Gauri Pinto's numerous cats and dogs that she nurtures back to health so assiduously after rescuing them from the streets of Pondicherry.

Our initial conversation centered around the rather violent cyclone that had just touched down in Pondicherry in November 2000 just a few days prior to my arrival on December 4th. My first rickshaw ride through the Government Park was startling; it resembled a war zone. All the leaves on the trees appeared to have been burned and most trees were barren and empty of greenery rendering the heat from the scorching sun all the more intense. Limbs were down everywhere and trees had toppled into the walls surrounding the governor's mansion as well as other buildings and houses.

Leaves, limbs and branches were burning on the corners of the streets filling the air with a billowing, acrid, choking cloud of smoke. Gauri said that the winds were so powerful that all the moisture was drawn from the leaves. The Ashram lost almost all of its "Transformation" trees. The winds, reaching up to 100mph, churned up the waves from the Bay of Bengal with such force that stones were sent hurling from the retaining wall clear across the beach boulevard as though a battle had been launched. That road had to be closed off to traffic and pedestrians for more than eight hours. It was the worst storm to hit the area in thirty years. Ashramites spoke of the Kali Yuga in connection with the cyclone.

As we began our interview Gauri served my favorite drink; "Power Syrup", made in the Ashram. It is a blend of the essences of hibiscus flowers, rose petals and lemon juice diluted in water with some sugar added. The drink was introduced to me in 1968 by the Pinto family. It is a most refreshing, cooling drink in the tropics.

Gauri told me that she was born Judy Ann Pinto on 16th November 1937 to Mona and Laurence (Udar) Pinto. They had just had their first darshan of the Mother and Sri Aurobindo a few months earlier. The Mother had requested that the baby should be born in the hospital in Bangalore where Udar's aunt was a doctor. There were no good hospitals in Pondicherry at that time. After six weeks time in Bangalore she was brought home to Pondicherry but was a fragile child and prone to sickness in her early years. She said she was surrounded by so many Tamil amahs from the beginning that she learned very early in her childhood how to speak the Tamil language fluently. There was much concern over the new baby's health as she was not taking her food properly and was way underweight for her age. She did not sleep well during the night and naturally kept her parents awake and concerned. Doctors were consulted and Udar and Mona entered into correspondence with the Mother regarding the matter. When the baby was about two months old Udar wrote asking if he could bring her to the Mother. The Mother replied," I do not find it prudent, still, to bring the child into the Ashram atmosphere. It is better to wait one year more." This practice actually became a rule in the Ashram. Babies and infants were not allowed to go as they could very easily feel and absorb the power and could not support the force.

Gauri showed me a large envelope filled with correspondence that had been sent to the Mother seeking advice and help in connection with her eating problem. In many instances Sri Aurobindo would answer as the Mother was so busy organizing the Ashram. In answer to one letter Sri Aurobindo replied, "Have you tried Horlicks Malted Milk Powder?"! (Horlicks is a British product, popular in India at that time and to date.) In another letter Mona states that the doctor advised that she starve-feed the baby. This meant withdrawing the feedings until she became really hungry and on a settled schedule. Sri Aurobindo responded, "The Mother does not approve of starve-feeding the child." (All of this correspondence was so very touching to me as here was the avatar, Sri Aurobindo, who brought down *The Life Divine*, *Savitri* and other profound words straight from The Source, giving out loving advice for a little baby who wouldn't eat!) A. B. Purani, a close friend of the family, also became involved and offered his parental advice and wisdom on childcare. Eventually her eating habits became normalized and she gained the proper weight. Gauri told me that Ambu, the late Ashram hatha yoga teacher, (to whom the Mother addressed her letters "To My Faithful Baby") was her "nanny"! "Ambu looked after me, gave me oil baths, fed me and took

Ambu in Hatha Yoga pose, Ashram 1983

me for walks while my parents worked for the Mother", Gauri said.

> *What was your earliest recollection of the Mother and Sri Aurobindo? What were you told about the Mother in early childhood and when did you realize she was someone special, not like everyone else?*

When we used to go for the balcony darshans when I was still very small I would say "Big Mama is coming, Big Mama is coming". I was brought up essentially with no religion. I was very close to nature and animals. When I thought of God I saw Sri Aurobindo's image. Also, I did not think of the Mother as a human being. It wasn't planned out for me that she would appear as a Goddess, but that's how it was in actuality. The Mother told my mother that I was a very old soul. When we would go up to see Mother on Darshan days she was like a mother to all of us. She taught us children so much. We would sit down before her and she would pat us on the head. We would go to the Mother and have lunch with her. The queues were long waiting to see Sri Aurobindo. We would see him four times a year. I saw him up to the age of thirteen at which time he left his body in 1950. He was for me the personification of Compassion. There was always so much light around him. I always saw this light around him and a loving, compassionate smile on his face.

Once I was bitten on the face by a dog and had become very frightened of all dogs after that experience. My father's aunt came to visit and felt it was not good for me to be so scared of dogs. Next visit she brought me a Dalmatian puppy.

I was so scared of it that I jumped on the table to get away from it, but eventually I grew to love it. The Mother named the dog "Spotted Beauty". When it was time for "Spotted Beauty" to be mated the Mother arranged for the dog to go to "visit" her friend, Madame Baron, the wife of the French governor of Pondicherry. They had a male Dalmatian so "Spotted Beauty" went to live in the governor's mansion! She gave birth to a litter of seven pups. I took them to the Mother and she was so charmed by the dogs that she took all 7 into Sri Aurobindo's room. He did not touch them but watched them run about. One pup, however, went and sat at Sri Aurobindo's feet and stared up at him with a transfixed expression. Mother said, "That is the one Gauri should keep." Mother named it "Beau".

> *Did you have other children to play with? The Ashram school had not been established when you were of school age. Where did you go to school and what was it like for you?*

When my father was sent to New Delhi by Sri Aurobindo in 1941 (from March to October) to work for the war effort, I was sent to a modern school there at the age of three years for a few months. My father told the Mother that he felt I needed some formal education. I had mostly only been around adults up to that point. When we came back to the Ashram from New Delhi, I was approaching four years of age. The Mother put me with an Englishwoman named Pavita. She was a very strict woman who used to go out and sweep the streets of Pondicherry! She had been the secretary to Paul Brunton.

[Paul Brunton was an occult journalist and author. He wrote *A Search in Secret India*. He wanted to interview the Mother and Sri Aurobindo and the Mother said, "If we see him he must not write anything about us." From what I was told he did get to see them but never wrote anything about them. He did, however, travel among sadhus, visited Ramana Maharshi's Ashram, wrote another book called *Secret Egypt*, then some other philosophical books.]

Pavita was the first teacher I remember and it was not a good experience. I remember her as being rather stern and strict. She wanted me to be a genius and pushed me too hard. It killed my creativity. She did not have bad will, she just did not know how to handle small children. In fact, she later became a good teacher in the Ashram school when it started on December 2, 1943. When the school opened I was in a classroom with other children and it was so good to finally be with other children. The Mother, herself, would often read stories to us during her Wednesday evening classes in the Playground. She would characterize each animal and character in such a charming, loving way.

However, one drawback for me when I began school was that I was held back in a class with smaller, younger children as I did not want Pavita to be my teacher any longer.

Could you further elaborate on why this was a drawback?

Well, I developed a bit of a complex being older and taller than the other children in my class and I didn't try very hard.

When and how was your name changed from Judy Ann to Gauri?

Although I was very timid, I loved to dance and particularly loved Indian dancing. I used to go to the library and listen to music. Whenever I heard music I would begin to dance freely. I chose two people at the library to dance with me and I wore anklets with bells. I would change my name every day. One day I would be "Jasmine", the next day "Lakshmi" and so on. My mother and I used to go to the Mother each night before the meditations. One by one we would stand before the Mother. I would lift Mother's sari slightly so that I could see the anklets that she was wearing. I would tell the Mother my name for that day. I was around five or so then. I loved beautiful flowers and Mother kept tiny-sized "Psychological Perfection" flowers in a glass bowl next to her. The Mother taught me how to do math by putting the flowers into my hand, taking away one then adding two or three more. The Mother would look at my hands and say "Mains de poupée" (hands of a doll).

[Gauri is a tall, willowy woman with a very refined and delicate face and hands and feet.]

One day I asked Mother for a name. She said, "I will give you a name if you promise you won't change it. I'll think about a name for you." Mother would determine the inner quality of a person and the meaning of the name she wanted to give that person, then she would ask Sri Aurobindo to give the appropriate name in Sanskrit.

Later on I went to the Mother with Ambu and after pranam Mother gave me the name Gauri ("The Fair One"). Mother said she did not mean fair in terms of my skin but rather she wanted the name to convey "inner fairness", the quality of being fair. It was a very serious moment and Mother's eyes were so powerful as she looked into me. Then she said "Gauri" with the "au" pronounced like the French "o".

How did the tradition of celebrating Christmas develop in the Ashram?

The first Christmas we celebrated was in 1938 when I was just one year old. It took place in our house called "The Red House". The guests were Nishtha (Margaret Woodrow Wilson), Ambu (our very close friend, the young hatha yoga teacher who looked after Nishtha) and François Sammer (one of the architects for Golconde). Nishtha made a big star to place on the top of the tree that year. Later, in 1943, when other children joined the Ashram, the Mother asked my mother to arrange the event for all the children. The Red House lawn was used and we arranged games, prizes and gifts for the children. Hats were made and everyone wore a paper hat. All were made by Golconde residents. Even special crowns were made for the Mother and Sri Aurobindo! Dyuman used to come out into the streets and blow a trumpet on Christmas day and a special hat was also made for him. When we moved to "Fenêtres" on Rue St. Gilles the celebration continued there and when the house got too small we shifted to the playground where the Mother came, herself, to distribute the gifts to all the children and grown-ups. Finally when the theatre was bought by the Ashram, the celebration was held there and the Mother came to give

Mother in the 1950s in the Ashram Theatre
on Christmas day

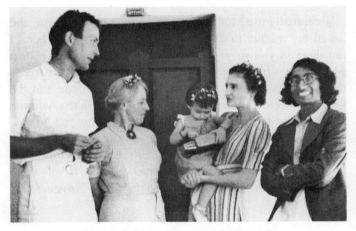

First Christmas 1938 with Mr. Sammer,
Margaret Woodrow Wilson, Mona and Baby Gauri and Ambu

out presents and to admire the tree and all the decorations.
The Mother gave importance to Christmas. She told us that
the initial celebration had come from the ancient Chaldean
tradition. [The Chaldeans were a people who lived in the
region of south-western Asia (Mesopotamia) on the Euphra-
tes River and among whom astrologers and magicians flour-
ished.] The wise men of that time observed that the calendar
days toward the end of the year were growing shorter and
shorter (the winter solstice) and people became worried that
they would be engulfed in darkness. Then they began to
notice that around the end of the month the days had begun
to grow longer and that there was a return of the light.
Christ's birth date ultimately became fixed to this time of
year as a symbol of the "return of the light".

Eventually the Mother stopped coming to the theatre and asked my mother to distribute the gifts. She said to her, "I am there in you so you do it instead." The chair on which Mother sat is placed in front of the tree each year. The tree is decorated by the residents and staff at Golconde and the Christmas celebration remains a joyous event in the Ashram. We continue to distribute gifts to all ashramites and guests.

[Mona Pinto told me that the Mother sent out the following letter to all ashramites for Christmas in 1972. It was to be her last Christmas before she left her body in November of 1973.

"Father Christmas,

I invoke you today. Answer our call. Come bearing all your marvellous gifts. You are the great dispenser of worldly possessions. You are the untiring friend who hears every request and grants it generously. Give each one the material object of his desires and as for me, give me enough, give me much, so that I may give largely to all."

Mother Mira

Christmas 1972

To the gifts of gold, frankincense and myrrh, brought to the Christ-child by the Magi, the Mother gave the following meanings:
Gold — Wealth of the world and Supramental Knowledge.
Frankincense — Purification of the vital.
Myrrh — Immortalization of the body.]

Gauri, who were your teachers in the upper grades in the Ashram school? What are your memories of those days and what can you explain of the Free Progress System?

Sunil-da was my botany teacher and he was absolutely wonderful. He was so innovative and imaginative. Tehmiben was also an excellent teacher. I learned many things from her. Mother once said to the teachers, "Why do you give exams?" Mother was very much against testing and homework so the Free Progress System was introduced, but Mother said, "It is not for everyone, it is only meant for those who are capable and have the discipline to study on their own and decide what it is that they want to do." The Free Progress System has been a bit chaotic and has not always been properly implemented. It is still in the process of development after all these years. Most teachers develop their own methods of teaching from within and from their own inspirations.

Did you ever want to go outside the Ashram and experience the outside world or marry and have children?

I first went outside the Ashram in 1968, with my mother, to visit relatives in London. The Mother said that going outside the Ashram would "enlarge my consciousness" and it has. I travelled again to London in 1975, 1986 and 1990, but the Ashram is my home and the Ashram life is my way of life so considering the worldly life and marriage was never an option for me.

You have been a teacher in the Ashram school for forty-five years. Could you share some details of that experience?

Becoming a drawing and English teacher was a turning point in my life. It helped to rid me of my timidity and helped me to gain confidence in myself. It is difficult to be a teacher in the Ashram. One must always be in control of one's vital impulses (temper, emotions, etc.); one must be self-observing and act in a yogic manner at all times. It is necessary to remain aware that the work is being done for the Mother and that one isn't there just to teach subjects, but also to help awaken the child's psychic being and to awaken their senses to inner and outer beauty. All these years I have taught English grammar, reading, literature, creative writing, comprehensive poetry and drawing to students from eleven years up to fifteen years of age. The Mother strongly encouraged developing the child's artistic side and appreciation of beauty.

How is the school different today? What changes do you see?

It is actually better today on the whole. People were more conservative and a bit dull in the old days. Now most of the teachers are former students who grew up here and have had more experience and are more interesting teachers.

What significant changes do you see in the Ashram?

Well, specifically, Mother put so much emphasis on beauty; beauty in buildings and the crafting of things. One often wonders, now, if that is still the aim. Mother's guidance is so much missed in the area of aesthetics.

> *Would you speak about the inspirations you received from Mother's talks in the playground or any stories of Mother that you would like to share?*

The Mother inspired us all to strive to be better human beings. Every Wednesday, during her talks in the playground, she would give us a boost and encourage us to rise above ourselves. As teenagers we would often become easily upset and sensitive to injustices. Mother would look into our eyes and all the pain would disappear. We learned so many lessons from Mother. She taught us how to be grateful. She would receive and accept all the little gifts we made for her with so much love and gratitude, even if they weren't made very well, and would show us, by her reactions, how to properly receive gifts. Ambu used to tell a beautiful "gratitude" story about the Mother. Some young Bengali devotees were travelling by train from Calcutta to Pondicherry to see the Mother. Also travelling on the train in their compartment was a simple village man. When they spoke of the Mother in his presence the man was very moved. He asked them to bring an offering of one rupee from him to be given to the Mother. When they went to the Mother and told her the story and gave her the rupee she said with great seriousness, "How can I ever repay this man?" Once someone sent her a small sum of money along with a note saying, "Buy yourself a mango"! Although the Mother was not particularly fond of mangoes she sent for one and ate some bites of it to show her gratitude. Mother taught us to appreciate beauty in all its forms; the reading of *Savitri*, poetry, literature, music and art. She was such a model for all us children. She gave importance to everything. She taught us also just how important it is to take care of material objects and to treat them with respect. I used to stand before the Mother and marvel, wonder-struck, at her own beauty.

Once she sent me a birthday card that read:

"Avec mes bénédictions pour développer et faire fleurir son culte, pour la beauté dans tous les domaines. Dans la Lumière et la Joie."(With my blessings for the development, flowering and cultivation of beauty in all its domains. With Light and Joy.)

In teaching us the four aspects of the Divine Mother, the Mother said, "There is another aspect... love!" She said this emanation had already been born on earth. She did not give a name but left it to us to find out. Of course we all thought it was her. Her love brought everyone together here. Some personal examples for me of her love took place once during a performance of "Swan Lake", a play in the Ashram school. I fainted backstage and Mother came and took my hand and walked me up and down the area and hummed the most beautiful, soft, soothing melody to me. It brought me around and then I was fine. Another time she came to our house when I had typhoid fever. Dark forms had begun to envelop me. The Mother soothed my head and soon I recovered and there were no more nightmares.

Gauri with one of her cats
at "Fenêtres", Dec. 2000

*What would you say that living in the Ashram has
provided for you that you could not have received in
the outside world? In closing, can you assess your sixty-
three years of life here in the atmosphere of the Ashram?*

Definitely the environment of the Ashram is significant. The
feeling of belonging, being loved by the Mother, guided by
her and living by her example has meant a lot. As stated
earlier, she constantly encouraged us to reach higher and
higher in everything we did. She took the time and gave of
herself to everyone. All life for us here in the Ashram re-
volved around the Mother. To grow in her presence was the
gift. The aim was not money, nor wealth, but to grow inwardly was the constant focus. I am filled with tremendous

gratitude for this wonderful experience of being here at a time when the Lord and the Divine Mother were on the earth. It took me some years to absorb and assimilate all that she had taught and I am so grateful for the grace that her life here brought to all of us.

You are here at this moment, that is to say upon earth, because you chose it at one time — you do not remember it any more, but I know it — that is why you are here. Well, you must rise to the height of the task. You must strive, you must conquer all weaknesses and limitations; above all you must tell your ego: "Your hour is gone." We want a race that has no ego, that has in place of the ego the Divine Consciousness. It is that which we want: the Divine Consciousness which will allow the race to develop itself and the supramental being to take birth.

The Mother

Tehmi Masalawalla

Tehmi Masalawalla

Tehmi Masalawalla, a gifted poet, teacher, translator of Mother's *Questions and Answers* and Satprem's *Sri Aurobindo or the Adventure of Consciousness*, was one of the first to reside in the Sri Aurobindo Ashram's Golconde residence from as early as 1947. When I visited her room I was immediately struck by the atmosphere that prevailed. She seemed to live within a vast, internalized sea of calm and peace. Her energies are very inner-directed while outwardly she remains poised and dignified. Her ascetic room denotes a being that does not have the need to live enveloped by the clutter of material objects. Golconde, in any case, is a minimalist's ideal, but photos of Mother and Sri Aurobindo, her books and a small vase of flowers seem to be sufficient for Tehmi's needs. The name Tehmi dates back to a well-known lady, Tehmina, in Persian legend who was the wife of Rustom, one of the great warriors of ancient Persian history.

Tehmi was born on January 17, 1917 into a deeply religious Parsi family in Bombay. Her father found a brief French phrase, succinct and to the point, which he used to repeat often to the family and even hung on the wall of their home; it read "Sans dieu, rien" ("Without God, nothing")! Her father was a surgeon and took a post as Chief Medical Officer of the Bhopal Hospital in Bhopal, India. I mentioned to Tehmi that I remembered meeting her father in Golconde in 1968 and how elegant he was. She told me that the Mother had also commented on the aristocratic nature of her mother. Her mother was also a doctor and graduated from medical school in Ireland. Tehmi and her brother (who also became a doctor) were sent at ages 8 and 7 back to Bombay to live with their aunties as there were no good schools in Bhopal at that time.

In her childhood in Bhopal and during visits from Bombay, Tehmi recalls rich stories of her parents' home and their life there. Bhopal was a Muslim city before India's independence and the family lived in a large wing of the Begum's (female Muslim ruler's) palace. Tehmi and Kekushroo had ample room in which to run and play and used to scamper about freely on the large sweeping stairways and marbled balconies and hallways of the palace. She recounted how darbars (official assemblies) would often take place and sumptuous dinner parties were held for all the dignitaries of the time. The children were not allowed to attend but they would peek down from the balconies and view the viceroys and other important gentlemen in their official attire as well as ladies wrapped in gold-trimmed saris and jewels as they entered the palace. Tehmi said the streets were sometimes filled with parades of camels and that the Nawab (Begum's son) had a stable of beautiful Arabian horses that were also often paraded through the streets during times of pageantry and festivals.

Tehmi went to Queen Mary School in Bombay and was finely trained in the arts, academics and gymnastics by the excellent English teachers who taught there. She told me that she excelled academically achieving the highest marks as she had an innate and natural ability to concentrate. She studied English literature at Saint Xavier's College in

Bombay and was taught there by many of the Jesuit fathers. She obtained degrees at Bombay University. After graduation she taught literature at Sophia College in Bombay.

> *The Parsis I have met are all highly refined people and very developed in the fields of art, music, literature, poetry, the sciences, etc. Do you attribute these special qualities as having come from the practice of the Zoroastrian faith? If so, what is it in the religion that allows for this special development so prevalent among Parsis? Zubin Mehta, the internationally famous conductor and musician comes to mind as one example plus all the fine Parsi poets, including yourself and Amal here in the Ashram.*

It is because of the Parsi symbolic worship of fire. The religion has a direct contact with the Divine with no intermediaries. There is a deep aspiration to express purity. The purity of purpose gives power and clarity to the mind and the vital.

> *What do you mean by "worship of fire"? Could you briefly describe the doctrines of Zoroastrianism and tell something of the history of how it developed?*

The Parsis are described as fire worshippers because fire is their central symbol. The pure flame of God. There are fires burning in the temples at all times. The fires burn day and night and are never extinguished. The Zoroastrians fled Persia in search of religious freedom and came to the

Udwada section of Gujarat in India. They brought burning lamps with them from their temples in Persia on their ships that crossed the Arabian Sea. The ruler of Gujarat welcomed them and gave them religious refuge there. They promised to live as his own people. One of the Zoroastrian High Priests asked for a cup of milk that he then mixed with water. He said, "We shall live as one people just as this milk has been mixed with water." Zoroaster was one of the great prophets who lived during the Vedic period. He had written twenty-one or more books on various subjects such as asrology, astronomy and medicine as well as the scriptures that he had brought down. He went to a mountaintop for forty years and during his time there he practised Tapasya [spiritual discipline] and brought down great words of wisdom and spiritual knowledge. He began teaching and preaching in the courts of Persia and he and his teachings were highly revered and soon became widespread throughout the land.

How old were you when you first discovered Sri Aurobindo?

I did not discover Sri Aurobindo right away. At age fifteen I began to read Sri Ramakrishna and books on other Indian saints and mystics. Later on in my search my father discovered Sri Aurobindo and gave me some of his books to read. I was still teaching then at Sophia College, but first came to Pondicherry for a couple of visits. Some years after that, around 1948, I came to stay permanently and my parents joined me a few months afterwards.

Did you ever consider marriage and the family life?

By the age of sixteen I had immersed myself totally in the spiritual search and was fully committed to living that life. I did not consider marriage nor family and this came about quite naturally.

Would you describe your first darshan with Mother and Sri Aurobindo or share any of the darshan experiences you had with them?

I saw the Mother twice a day. She used to give darshan in the mornings in the meditation hall. In the evenings we would go up for darshan to the top of the staircase. I remember my first darshan of the Mother. I saw her sitting at the top of the stairs wearing the most exquisitely beautiful blue sari. Her eyes were something indescribable. I was overwhelmed by the experience. She took us over immediately. Sri Aurobindo's power was quite different. I saw him only when he gave darshans four times a year. We passed by him one by one very quickly but he transferred so much Force into each of us in such a short amount of time. I remember one April darshan in the afternoon sitting in the courtyard waiting to go upstairs. I could feel, palpably, the entire courtyard rocking back and forth from the amount of Force emanating from his presence. This is one of the reasons children were not allowed in the Ashram until a certain age. The force was too strong. They would often fall ill.

During my first darshan, as I was approaching the inner room, when I reached the door I could feel two rays of light entering my chest. I was still standing at the door when I felt this. When I stood in front of Sri Aurobindo it was as though I was in a trance and I walked away still in that state. Once, however, I was talking to the Mother prior to a darshan with Sri Aurobindo. I said, "Mother, I don't 'see' Sri Aurobindo during the darshans. Of course I see him physically, but I feel that I don't see him inwardly." The Mother said. "Yes, it is true, this is very difficult." "But Mother, others tell me that they 'see' him." She said, "Then, perhaps they are only pretending." After that next darshan I "saw" Sri Aurobindo in a totally different way. The Mother had opened my inner sight and given me the ability to truly "see" Sri Aurobindo.

What was it like to live in Golconde in those early days?

I felt it was such a blessing. Since it was called a "guest house" I thought surely Mother would put me somewhere else and when I went to her for an interview I asked her, "Where shall I stay now?" Mother said, "Why, you will continue to stay here in Golconde, Mona likes you very much." So, this has been my home for fifty-three years.

What work did the Mother give you in the early days and throughout your years in the Ashram?

I had grown very tired of my teaching post at Sophia College and was hoping that Mother would not give me a teaching assignment. I just kept saying, "Let Mother give me any other work!" So, she put me to work in the Carpentry Department supervising all the carpenters! I had a very nice boss and could see the ocean from my office. My boss said, "Mother wishes that one should not read nor meditate during work hours." So very often when I had no immediate work I would just sit and dream. I did this work for two years and then after that I worked in the library. I also did hand painting on cloth for Mother's saris and shawls and the special cards she gave to people. I mostly painted roses but also other flowers as well. One day, however, during pranam, the Mother asked me if I would take a class in the school. She had heard of my qualifications from some of the students. I accepted. She also put me to work for the *Bulletin of the Sri Aurobindo International Centre of Education*. It was clerical work taking care of postings, getting addresses ready and accounts for subscribers. I still do this work with some help from others. At this time I only take care of receipts and subscriptions. I was a teacher of poetry and prose and taught sixteen and seventeen year olds for twenty-five years.

> *How and when did the Mother give you the work of translating Satprem's* Sri Aurobindo or the Adventure of Consciousness?

When Satprem finished the book in French, Mother expressed a wish to have it translated into English. Jayantilal, with whom I worked in the *Bulletin* office, heard about this and told me about it. He asked me if I would be interested. He asked the Mother about it and she said, "Yes, she can do it." I had done my B.A. in French literature and had read many of the major French writers in the French language. I

Tehmi's Painting

had also translated Mother's *Entretiens* into English.

> *Did you have many meetings with Satprem regarding the book?*

I had many meetings with Satprem, probably eighteen or more times in all. He was very pleased with the translation and quite overwhelmed. He would go to the Mother with my work with praises about the translation. I also did the work very rapidly. He used to come to Golconde and go over everything with me.

> *Satprem once told me that Sri Aurobindo dictated every word of* The Adventure of Consciousness *through him and that he "just held the pen". Did you have a similar experience with the translation?*

Yes, Mother and Sri Aurobindo were all the time with me. The Mother had told me that she and Sri Aurobindo would help me with the work. I could feel the help coming from above my head as I was engaged in the translating.

> *Did you translate other works of Satprem?*

I translated his book *La Genèse du Surhomme* (*On the Way to Supermanhood*) and after that there were no other translations of his works done by me.

> The Adventure of Consciousness *was a very important book for Americans in the 1960s and brought many*

people to the yoga. I still recommend the book for new-comers to the yoga although I miss your translation that is out of print. When the book first came out in 1964 the New York distributor sent a copy to my home in New York City with a note enclosed that read "At the behest of the Mother"! It opened and widened my consciousness and was just the right book at the right time.

Is there a difference in the atmosphere of the Ashram since Mother and Sri Aurobindo left their bodies?

There is no real difference. The presence is still very power-ful. I feel it everywhere. Some people feel that the Force has dispersed, but it is very vital, very alive.

Is there a disadvantage in never having seen Mother and Sri Aurobindo in their physical bodies?

It is difficult for me to judge this, really. It meant so much to have the Mother's personal touch on a daily basis. She had so many ways of training our consciousness from the inside out. One was elevated to new heights and turned inside out by her. What power there was in her eyes and in her smile! Sri Aurobindo said that the Mother worked on people through her eyes and smile.

In what way has your sadhana changed since the Mother left her body?

For me the sadhana has remained the same. However, in the

early years all the work we did was done for the Mother and her alone. The Mother had given us our work and all our work was dedicated to her. No one questioned this, it was simply the natural way and the thing to be done. In the evenings we would go where the Mother was, to see her play tennis; she taught classes in French and watched us do gymnastic marching. She participated in all of the life of the ashramites and students from early morning balcony darshan until evening time.

Have you faced many difficulties in your sadhana and how do you deal with such difficulties?

Yes, naturally there have been difficulties. Human nature is not so wonderful. Prayer is essential. Always pray to the Mother for help. Also one should look at oneself clearly and honestly in order to set things right in one's being. Only with her help and power and presence can one come through such times. In the early days when we were younger, often when the difficulties seemed insurmountable, we used to go to the Mother about the problems and she would set everything right again.

What changes do you see taking place in the future of the Ashram and will it be very different from what it is now?

I do not see any fundamental changes taking place. Surface changes will be there, but at the core the people who sincerely practice the yoga will keep things going as the Mother would have it.

*Now that you have reached almost eighty-four years,
what has the yoga done for you at this stage in your
life?*

To live constantly in the consciousness of the Divine, to
live consciously with the Mother and in the Mother at all
times, no matter what I am doing, what I am thinking, has
been the goal. To know that it is all her doing and not ours
and that she is molding us and shaping us and will not turn
away from us. That has been my constant experience all
these years and remains so. That is why I have always been
reluctant to go outside the Ashram or Pondicherry. Some
friends have taken me to the Lake Estate but that is as far as
I have gone in fifty-three years. I do not wish to go out. I
have found complete fulfilment in the Ashram life and am
absolutely happy here. I do not have many visitors now.
Mostly people come to me in connection with the work that
I am still doing. I do not even have, at this stage in life, very
much of a sense of the personal "I" or the individualized
self left in me. I am now prepared to accept and become
whatever Mother chooses for me.

*How did you receive the inspiration to write your poems
and the mystery play that you wrote entitled Demeter
and Persephone?*

I wrote poetry in Bombay before coming to the Ashram. It
was on my poetry from this period that Sri Aurobindo gave
his comments and some of the poetry of my early years in
the Ashram. The poetry used to come quite easily. The lines

came to me during work and while doing ordinary things and I would then sit down and put the lines on paper. It was never forced. Some poems came in two or three line stanzas or quatrains.

> *When I read your book of poetry I found the poems to be filled with great passion, feelings and emotions as if the poet was describing a love affair with the Divine.*

This is quite so, that is how it was.

Tehmi in her room at Golconde Dec. 2000

*Sri Aurobindo has made comments on your poetry and
so has Amal Kiran. In closing I am going to add to the
interview four of your beautiful poems from your book
of poetry and the comments made by Sri Aurobindo
and Amal on your poems.*

Your Word

Your word comes singing to my soul
And passes over night's silent sea;
I cannot keep it or control
Or capture all it says to me.

But the deep caves resound with light,
The terraces of being flame,
And everywhere from depth to height
Reverberates your beauteous Name.

The earth a-tremble to the core
Bursts open its vast granite hold,
Releasing through its broken floor
Strange sacred fountains flowing gold.

Gift

Beloved, you bring to me
  Beauty beyond compare:
The pure, white ecstasy —
  The hour of silent prayer.

The wells of light unclose
　Beneath your touch of flame;
All memories repose
　Regathered in your name.

My muted thoughts evolve
　Swift wings of golden fire;
Within your breath dissolve
　All darkness and desire.

The heavens unfold above,
　Eternities of grace;
Resplendent worlds of love,
　Mirrored within your face.

Krishna's Coming

Around my heart I set gold trellis,
　And hung the roof with filligree,
For Krishna of the myriad splendours
　Was coming with his pageantry;

I wove golden fairy-netting,
　And worked it in with jewelry,
For Krishna of the shining joy-songs
　Was coming in his pomp to me.

Ah, everything and everywhere
　I decked with pearl and diamond lace,

With exquisite and quiet care
 To fashion a chamber for his Grace.

When all was ready, the fire bright,
 Love's silent sacrificial flame,
I sat within its rapturous light
 Awaiting him. And...yes, He came.

Beyond the Word

Beyond the wordiness of the word,
 Beyond its pomp and show,
Where the crystal meaning sings a bird
 On the hills of truth, I'd go.

I'm tired of all this trumpery,
 Fine phrases void of heart,
Vain peacockings of majesty,
 The God-king's regal art.

O sweet beloved simplicity,
 White wisdom of the soul,
Your purifying radiance free
 To pass across my scroll.

O Word of God, immaculate,
 From silences deep heard,
From inward pureness liberate
 In me the truth-born word.

          TEHMIS

The Mother had told Tehmi to use Themis, the name of the Greek goddess of Justice and Law for the publication of her poems and her play *Demeter and Persephone*.

The following are Sri Aurobindo's comments conveyed through Nirodbaran after the latter read Tehmi's poems to him:

"The poems are remarkable, especially the later ones. They have power of revelatory image and phrase and of expressing spiritual experience. Also, her later poems are very remarkably built, the thought is worked out in a perfect beginning, middle and end in a way in which is not very common. Many poems contain a beautiful lyrical quality.

"The early poems too are very powerful expressions of the kind of experience she had and as poetry hardly inferior to the later ones. There are many remarkable lines and stanzas though they are not as well-built as the later ones."

The following are Amal Kiran's comments:

"You are a very fine poet. You have a genuine gift spontaneously sustained over years and some of your pieces are absolutely first-rate quality. And this quality is not only exquisiteness: there is a distinct vein of what must be called greatness — that is to say, the thought, the vision, the emotion have both weight and depth and are carried to us on a rhythmic tone bringing a touch of some infinite which suggests a beyond to all that can be uttered. Often, your expression is, as you have put it in your letter to me, "quiet" — but nobody can mistake your quietness for absence of the stately, the wide-ranged, the deep-plunging. No doubt, your style is mainly lyrical and not ostensibly epical, nor are you markedly dynamic as a rule but there can be not only lyrical largeness coupled with intensity but also a lyricism quietly commanding as well as intense and such lyricism can, in addition, keep mostly its exquisiteness in front without ceasing to offer its own greatness."

Yet, in the blindness of Matter itself there are signs of a concealed consciousness which in its hidden fundamental being sees and has the power to act according to its vision and even by an infallible immediacy which is inherent in its nature. This is the same Truth that is apparent in Supermind but is here involved and seems not to be.

Sri Aurobindo

Sunanda

Sunanda Poddar

(Caretaker of "Srismriti", The Mother's Museum)

Sunanda Poddar has lived in the Sri Aurobindo Ashram since the age of sixteen with the exception of eight years in East Africa where she worked for SABDA (Sri Aurobindo Book Distribution Agency). Her name, given by her parents and unchanged by the Mother, means "Full of Happiness". Early on, the Mother devoted much time to and showed great interest in this engaging and charismatic woman. Sunanda is the author of books and plays of fairy tales for children, and was a teacher in Auroville and the Ashram school. She worked with her husband, the late Balkrishna Poddar, at SABDA in the Ashram and in East Africa. Sunanda is a clairvoyant and pranic energy healer working with crystals and since 1989 she has been the caretaker of "Srismriti", the Mother's Museum. Here begins her extraordinary story:

> *Where were you born and what was your family life like? Were your parents spiritual or religious people?*

I was born in Nairobi, Kenya, on February 24, 1934. I was born into a family immersed in the inner, spiritual life and my aunt performed routine Hindu religious ceremonies in her little temple. Before moving to Africa both of my parents had worked for the freedom movement with Mahatma

Gandhi at the grass-roots level in the villages of Gujarat.
They dispensed medicines where there had been floods and
other problems such as epidemics, etc. They had both become devotees of Mother and Sri Aurobindo in the late
1920s and in 1929 they moved to Nairobi where my father's
brother was living. They had visited the Ashram long before I was born. They did not perform religious rites in our
home but meditation was a daily part of family life. My
father, Shivabhai Amin, was a lawyer and had his own office and practice in Nairobi.

> *What were your special talents? Did they manifest early
> in your childhood?   What were your childhood
> ambitions and dreams?*

I was influenced by my parents' love of work with the freedom movement in India. I dreamed of becoming a doctor
and settling in a village in India where there was no doctor
so that I could treat the unfortunate free of charge. I was
very idealistic.

> *Were you aware of a spiritual presence in your
> childhood? When did you first begin to aspire deeply
> for the spiritual life?*

I loved the religious ceremonies my aunt performed and I
joined her in fasting and worship of the idols in her small
temple. My parents did not want me to go to the temples but
explained to me that God listened to your prayers at home,
or in school or on the road or whenever you called sincere-

ly. My family did not have much of a social life and I did
not have many playmates in childhood. I loved the garden
in our home and as a child I entered into fantasy play there
and had long conversations with flower fairies and the
God, Shiva, who became my personal God. This life was so
real to me that I thought everyone had a similar inner life.
As I grew up, I realized that in my life with the fairies and
Shiva I was not like everyone else, so there was a remote
search for something of which I was not fully aware at that
time. The fairies were to remain with me for my lifetime
but Shiva was ultimately replaced by the Mother and Sri
Aurobindo.

> *When did you come to the Ashram for the first time and*
> *when did you have darshan of Sri Aurobindo and the*
> *Mother?*

It was in 1942 and I was eight years old. I came with my
parents and I was so taken with the Mother's beauty, her
love, the flowers everywhere and the quiet, nightly meditations under the service tree. I wanted to stay and go to the
school that Mother was forming at that time, but there was
not as yet a boarding facility and neither of my parents could
stay with me there, so we had to return to Africa. I had
darshan of Sri Aurobindo that August 1942 but I don't
remember how he looked. I remember the garlands we carried for the Mother and the Tulsi (basil) garlands for Sri
Aurobindo. The predominant feeling for me then was that
of a very special event at a very special place where I felt
that I wanted to be.

When did you return for your final stay?

I returned in 1951 when I was just sixteen. My father had
sent me to the Ashram on a visit specifically to ask the
Mother if I should take up medicine or law for my further
education. I so much wanted to be a doctor but my father
wanted me to take up law. I had left home on my own for the
first time and was staying in Golconde. In fact, I was the
youngest person to ever stay in Golconde. The first day I
went for the Mother's darshan she gave me a flower and
smiled so sweetly. In the evening in the playground I stood
with the visitors. As the Mother distributed prasad she asked
me, "Don't you want to join the other children in exercises?"
I said, "Yes, Mother, I'd like to." She said, "Tomorrow you
give your measurements for shorts and shirts." That next
evening one pair of shorts and a shirt were given to me and
my new life began without my even knowing about it or
deciding about it on my own. This truly shows the greatness
of the Mother. I joined a group but was not yet in school.
Every day I would go to the library which was in the main
Ashram compound then. Vasanti-di was working there at
that time. She would see me every day reading poetry and
books. Then in the afternoons I would go wherever I could
see or be near the Mother.

*Could you describe what it was like to be in the Mother's
presence in those days?*

The Mother used to dress in a long gown with matching
scarf on her head. When she came out on the terrace outside

her room the time was between 10 and 11a.m. Her close companion, Chinmayee, carried a parasol to protect the Mother's head from the scorching sun. A crow would invariably come and hop onto the ledge of the terrace. Chinmayee would hand over some biscuits to the Mother who in turn would feed them to the crow! I mostly looked at her lovely pastel — colored clothes and matching parasols and her lovely smile. In the evenings when she would give darshan at the head of the staircase, she was like a goddess from the scriptures. She wore saris and embroidered bands over her forehead. She looked taller than when I saw her during the mornings. She radiated light, light and more light. She received our flowers and we bowed down to her feet. She looked into our eyes and smiled down on us as we looked up at her. Often her smile was like a silent laugh. She gave us some flowers and then we came down the staircase. I did not want to look at anyone because her image was in my eyes and I wanted to hold on to it for as long as I possibly could. By 1951 things were quite different. The school and many other workshops were functioning at that time. The playground was a must for everyone. There were many more people then than when I first came in 1942. Mother would come down to play tennis at 4 p.m. She would come down the staircase and look at us and smile. Her smile was very important to us. She would get into her Humber car with Pavitra driving. I would run as fast as I could to the tennis grounds with Pavitra driving slowly alongside so that I could see Mother arriving and getting out of the car, then we would all sit and watch her play tennis.

*When did you become officially connected to the
Ashram and begin your classes in the school?*

After I had been in the Ashram for two months an interview
was arranged for me by my father's friend, Dyuman. My
father had written to him that I had been in the Ashram for
all this time and had not written home. It was to be my initial personal interview. I sat on the ground and the Mother
sat on a low chair. "What would you like to ask?" Mother
said. Instead of asking her if I should study law or medicine
I found myself asking her if I should stay in the Ashram or
go out of the Ashram to study. She said, "What do you want
to do in life?" I told her that my father wanted me to study
law but that I wanted to study medicine. Mother said, "We'll
forget about law because you are not interested in it." She
asked me in great detail why I wanted to study medicine. I
told her that it was not for money but that I wanted to help
the poor, unfortunate people of India for no charge. I told
her that I had a great love for India and that Shiva was my
personal god. The Mother said, "I can see that you would
make a good doctor, but what I see today you may not be
aware of and you may lose that if you go out of the Ashram."
I said, "Mother, if I stay, will you accept me?" She said,
"But I have already accepted you." In those days gold was
given for its inner qualities of warmth and purity, the money-
oriented reasons came later. I had two bangles, a chain and
earrings and I placed these in her lap. I had no money and
no other valuables to give her. That was the moment when
becoming an ashramite was final. Mother said, "I will arrange for you to study medicine here."

This was so amazing to me because there was only one hospital in Pondicherry at that time...the General (Government) Hospital. So, Mother went to Nirodbaran and asked him to teach me medicine! The Mother told him to do this and he did it. Then she said that I was to go to the main Ashram school as well. Nirodbaran gave me a huge, monstrous book to read on anatomy (this was all such a humorous thing). He said, "Here, you read this" and I did it because Mother said to do it! I sat on the parapet near the samadhi with this ages-old edition (probably the one he used from the early 1900s) and religiously read page after page of the book. (Dyuman had finally written to my father that I was staying in the Ashram.) This study went on for a few months and after some time Nirodbaran gave it up. Dr. Sen joined the Ashram and opened a clinic to treat students injured in the playground. After group I would work with him helping people who had got hurt at the playground. Finally, Dr. Sanyal was given the job of training all the students interested in medicine. He took seven of us to the General Hospital to see a dead body and to view the internal organs. I think this is what ended my interest in medicine. I was around eighteen or so during this period.

You visited Mother on a regular basis for quite some time. How did you receive this special blessing?

There were three photographs in the Ashram reception. One on the east side, one on the west side and one in the center of the room. In the photo on the left hand side, I could not see Sri Aurobindo, I could only see Shiva. I would rub my eyes and open and close them in disbelief. I was feeling quite guilty about this as I had accepted Mother and Sri Aurobindo as my gurus and felt that I should only worship them and not Shiva. I was also continuing to fast on Mondays. A girl from my group had asked me to have lunch with her. I told her I was not taking food. She gave me quite a lecture about not being faithful and that I was worshipping old deities. I was so ashamed. At pranam I told Mother that I wanted to see her. I mentioned my situation and she listened very carefully. She asked me details about my worship of Shiva. I told her of my childhood in the garden and how I had grown up with Shiva. I asked her to help me see Sri Aurobindo. She had a small book by her table. She opened the book at random and said, "Here, read this." The sentence was by Sri Aurobindo telling someone in a letter, "Shiva and I are one." The Mother said, "Don't worry about things, slowly a time will come when you will call us. She said, "It will be Ma, Shiva, Ma, Shiva at first." Then I made a concerted effort to switch. I sat for meditation, then it happened and it was no longer disturbing to me. She also asked me other details of what I experienced when I was quiet and on my own. At that time I told her of the visions that I saw at times. She asked me if I still had these visions and I told her that I saw many things. She asked me to write down things as I experienced them and to send them to her. She said if sometimes I had something special to tell her that I should come to her room in the mornings before school. She wanted to help me give meaning and explanations to my experiences. I went to her room every day after that from 1952 to 1954. I would tell her of my visions. Sometimes I would go and spend time by the sea in the evenings. Once I saw an impression of the Mother's feet in the sand. I started praying that the tide would not roll in and wipe out the impression. Suddenly the impression rose above the ground and into the air. When I related this to the Mother she smiled and was silent. A few months later on my birthday, along with flowers, there was a bundle wrapped in cloth given to me by the Mother. It was a pair of her gold brocade chappals that had been made in the Ashram. I knew that this was connected with my vision on the beach and that she had given them to me as a result of that experience. So much was communicated through the Mother without the use of words. There would be an understanding of what was to be said through a flower you gave or that She gave to you. I then began to speak to Mother about the fairies that I had been seeing since childhood. She would sometimes just listen and at other times explain things.

[Sunanda, did not even know what the word clairvoyant meant at that age, but she is one and she also has the gift of seeing auras and working with pranic energy. She can scan the body for diseases, blockages and imbalances.]

Could you share something of your voyage into the world of fairies and how your fairy stories and plays were published?

I was staying in Golconde and each day I would write about what had happened in my dreams and experiences. I would write during the night and in the morning would tear the pieces of paper up and throw them in the wastepaper-basket in my room at Golconde. One day Mona came and said, "What is it that you are tearing up to such an extent and throwing away?" I was so embarrassed. I went to the Mother and told her that something pushes me to write and then I tear everything up and throw it away. "Anything coming to you like this is not your writing and you have no business to tear it up and throw it away. Write everything down and bring it to me." So, that started another step in my connection with the Mother. I took my writings to her every day. After a few days she said there were some nice things in the papers. She said, "Why don't you tell stories to the children?" I asked her, "What stories should I tell? If they are fairy tales from the West then I can surely do that or Indian myths as well." Mother said "Neither; you will go to a class-room, sit there and any children who want to listen to your stories can go to that room. The stories will come to you and you will tell them to the children." There was such trepidation in my heart and I said, "Suppose they don't come to me?" But I agreed anyway and started telling the stories. I would have the experiences, write them down and the next day I would tell the stories. My writings were passed on to the Mother who gave them to Nolini. Nolini read them and found complete stories in them. Mother told him to separate the ones that could be published. There were no books for children in the Ashram at that time.

One day in the playground (a famous date 23-4-56) Mother was giving prasad. She caught my hand and said, "Wait here." Why she had stopped me I did not know. Someone went inside and brought out a newly published book titled *Stories and Plays for Children* and on the cover was my name at the bottom! My mother was so elated. I was just twenty-two years old. Balkrishna was there and had heard about the book. When I came away with the book I wondered how this could have happened. Balkrishna told me he saw it while it was being printed. All the while everyone knew about this but me! [Sunanda continued to write and publish stories for children.]

> *Are the fairies complete material formations? How do they look? Are they like extensions of the plant world?*

The fairies that I saw in the garden as a child never seemed to be a big deal to me. In fact, I thought everyone saw them. They actually had physical forms. They weren't all the time there. Sometimes I would see them and sometimes not. Yes, they generally looked like extensions of the plant world. They appeared as one would imagine flower fairies would look. They had wings on them and were always cloaked in pastel colors. I have never seen a fairy with very dark colors. Even the red ones were transparent with a lot of light play around them. They were always full of light and very luminous as if edged in light. They were often gold and silver. They were not even as large as a small baby. They were no bigger than around four to ten inches." This is not a permanent world, but always a changing, newly forming world.

> *Did the fairies wear actual clothing and do they have human-like faces? Do they speak? Do you still see them? Do you think that this world increased for you*

*after you told the Mother about the fairies? Are the
fairies the same as the beings called "devas" who
preside over gardens?*

Some fairies have human faces. Others have bird-like faces
or flower faces. Some had crowns made with subtle light
formations or flowers. The clothing was like gossamer, very
transparent like dragon-fly wings. They mostly communicated with feelings but sometimes talked among themselves.
I still see this world of fairies. They are the same entities as
"devas". They still come to me although I am practising
yoga. Now there is more meaning in them for me. I see them
as spirits of the vegetable kingdom — not just as playmates
any more. Not only did this world of fairies increase through
the Mother but a whole world of beauty, refinement and the
realization of her perfection in works was shown. Now I
call them "beings" — overseers of the vegetal kingdom.
Sometimes the larger "beings" take the smaller "beings"
into the tops of the trees. C. took a photo at Lake Estate. He
had it blown up and gave it to a friend as a birthday gift
because he took it in a beautiful spot at a lovely time of day
when the light was creating special effects on the ground. A
mutual friend saw the photo and found something "mysti-
cal" in it. She brought it to me for confirmation. I confirmed
the presence of fairies in the photo.

[I asked Sunanda to bring me the photo the next day. I
clearly saw the phenomenon. C. had definitely, although
unknowingly, captured something. Sunanda had to point out
some things but I saw many of these subtle images myself
and in some instances they were quite visible.]

What do you see as being the purpose for this extra-sensory sight that you have been given?

It has made me more aware of the consciousness of the subtle worlds. It has helped me to become more aware of the world around me as it relates to the worlds within. It has expanded my consciousness and even helps me when I heal people. It has given me an inner contact with plants and flowers and the entities behind them. It has put me in closer contact with the Mother. It is a gift from the Mother that has helped me to give meaning to my visions and contact with the inner worlds.

Have you ever seen Mother and Sri Aurobindo in the subtle worlds?

Yes, I have seen them on the subtle planes. They appear as human forms but when they "walk" they advance without taking steps. They move as though in a gliding motion over the subtle surfaces. Generally Sri Aurobindo is seen in white, blue and gold. The Mother has all the subtle pastel colors.

Can you share the story of your meeting with, marriage to and work with Balkrishna Poddar?

I was around twenty and teaching English in the Ashram school in the mornings. I asked the Mother for some additional work for the afternoons after school. Simultaneously, Balkrishna had asked the Mother for a helper at SABDA.

The Mother gave this work to me. I started keeping the accounts and was introduced to book sales work. Balkrishna and I developed a friendship. He had such a pure nature and was a most sympathetic man. Eventually marriage was discussed and we put this to the Mother who gave us the permission to marry. She asked us to open a SABDA branch in East Africa and to continue the book sales there. She said, "I will keep you as my children and will call you back to the Ashram. This arrangement will not be permanent." We remained there for eight years. Every two years we returned to the Ashram to report on the work to the Mother. For our upkeep we both took jobs in local schools as teachers. We moved around in our small Volkswagen through all the large towns and small villages with books on top of the carrier. We arranged exhibitions on the Ashram and gave talks at schools and temples and conference halls...just the two of us with no one else. We trudged through the jungles of Africa and with Mother's grace and protection we managed to escape a herd of charging elephants, swarms of locusts and serious floods along the way. It was quite an adventure.

When you returned to the Ashram after being in Africa, what did you do?

I taught in Auroville in the Last School. There were several of us graduates from the Ashram school who went out to Auroville three times a week and came back by 12:30 p.m. to the Ashram. The children were mixed ages; post kindergarten. I did this for one and a half years. Balkrishna had come back to continue his work for SABDA. I worked for SABDA in the background only. However, in 1974 I gave up teaching and went to work full-time for SABDA. I helped to establish the SABDA branch on Rue de la Marine. In August 1989 Nishtha's old flat became available and the Ashram decided to use it to display the articles of Mother and Sri Aurobindo. They put me in charge of the museum under the able advice of Jayantilal, Krishnalal and Vasudev.

Srismriti Museum

The Srismriti Museum is located in the large building across from the Ashram playground. It is quartered in the flat that was once occupied by Nishtha (Margaret Woodrow Wilson), the daughter of the 28th President of the United States. She had lived there in the late 1930s. Krishnalal, Sunanda and Jayantilal named the museum "Srismriti" which means "Sacred Remembrance" in Sanskrit.

Sunanda's keenly developed sense of taste and aesthetics is most obvious in the way in which she has arranged and set up the museum. She also takes the greatest care to keep all objects polished, clean and dust-free. It is a joy to see the case of small stuffed animals and tiny little animal figures in wood and porcelain, given as gifts by disciples to the Mother. They carry such a life force and all appear as though they are on the verge of moving. Their eyes even shine with a life-like sparkle. There is an indescribable charm in this unique little curio cabinet and the entire museum itself is a very special darshan experience. Sunanda would not allow me to take photographs inside but I would like to take everyone along

Sign at entrance to Srismriti Museum, Dec. 2000

Sunanda working at Srismriti

on a "virtual" verbal-description tour of all the precious objects that are housed there:

The first room is a long, rectangular room with about nine curio cabinets. There is an immense ornate chandelier hanging overhead that was given to the Mother by the royal family of Hyderabad. It once burned wick oil lamps but was converted to electricity. In the first cabinet there are small and large photos of the Mother, photos of the last few years of her balcony darshans bearing her original signatures, a Baroque glass platter from Europe with Mother's photo in the center, some of Mother's original sketches and a magnificent late 19th century French clock.

The second cabinet is a collection of blessings packets from the early days to date, articles used by the Mother, i.e. combs, hair-pieces and European perfume bottles.

The third cabinet holds postage stamps of Mother and Sri Aurobindo issued by the Indian Government.

The fourth cabinet includes saris and shawls used by the Mother when she was writing *Prayers and Meditations* in the Ashram; Mother's gold watch and Huta's painting of Mother at the organ.

In the fifth cabinet one finds French boxes, hand-painted cards, purses in brocaded fabric, usually containing money, given to Mother by affluent Indians.

The sixth cabinet holds paper-weights, clocks, hand-painted writing paper, desk calendars. One of the calendars had actually been used by the Mother and was opened to the pages of March and April of 1962. In it she had times set aside for Dimitri (Feb. 4, 1962) and Sam Spanier (March 12, 1962)! Also in the case is a Parker pen that was used by Sri

Aurobindo and later given to the Mother. There are some Egyptian scarab beetles and the head of a pigeon (both occult objects).

Number seven houses dishes and utensils used by Sri Aurobindo and the Mother. It also stores a fourteen-inch knife, made by Harpagon. It had been made especially for the Mother to cut her enormous 80th birthday cake!

Number eight is a case filled with beautiful saris.

Number nine holds stationery, book marks and notebooks used in Mother's French classes plus a Corona typewriter that was given to the Mother by Rabindranath Tagore while she was in Japan.

Also in this room is a stunning standing brass oil lamp with sixty-five wick lamps. On the top sits an ornate brass peacock. It was given by the poet and film star, Harindranath Chattopadhyay. This room also holds chairs used by the Mother and Sri Aurobindo before 1926.

The second room has eleven cabinets filled with offerings to Mother and Sri Aurobindo by disciples and the Mother's toy collection (wooden, papier mâché, clay and stuffed).

Mother-of-pearl shells, glass animals and Czechoslovakian and Russian dolls in ethnic dress are housed in this room. There are miniature elephants in varying sizes carved from ivory. Some are so miniscule that a magnifying glass is needed to identify the shapes. Jeweled Puja and ceremonial objects of worship — Vishnu on Garuda, chariots in ivory, Ganesh, Radha and Krishna in soapstone and other deities in wood and brass. Mother's baskets, chappals (Japanese), silver articles, geodes, stones and shells. There is a handsome teakwood sideboard, a Buddhist cabinet and articles made by Ashramites for Mother's use. A silk brocaded floral jacket in mango motif (Mogul style called Jamewar) given by the Hyderabad royal family. There are also articles given by the Mother for the theatre department such as make-up, crowns, old upholstery for cloaks and some spoons in silver and ivory.

The next room is a decorated setting using some of Sri Aurobindo's old furniture and belongings. There is a bed, a chair (in wicker with markings on it from Sri Aurobindo's head), clothing, a carpet, pens, paper-weights (made from elephant tusks), Sri Aurobindo's old typewriter (either a Remington or Underwood) that he used when preparing the *Arya* publications. There is also a footstool with indentations on it from Sri Aurobindo's feet, and a photo of Sri Aurobindo etched in glass. There are trays holding the earliest teacups that Mother used when she brought tea to Sri Aurobindo in the afternoons. There are dhotis, kurtas, shawls, bed covers (painted by sadhaks), screens from Burma and India. In this room there is also a steel trunk with brass fittings that Sri Aurobindo used when he sailed to Pondicherry after his acquittal in Calcutta. (Sri Aurobindo's acquittal took place in May 1909 and he arrived in Pondicherry in April 1910.)

The fourth and final room in the museum houses the Mother's exquisite Japanese collections. She used these beautiful articles in Japan as well as after her arrival in Pondicherry. There are some lovely writing papers and envelopes. The paper has preserved itself miraculously well for almost a century. The Mother was a very keen collector of bottles and boxes. This case contains her lacquer writing box, painting box and many other boxes with mostly black background and embossed designs in mother-of-pearl, shells, copper, brass and silver flowers and leaves. There is also a tea ceremony set. This room has gifts to the Mother of Japanese dolls, ceramic tea sets hand painted with gold powder, very fine examples of blue and white china-ware, many varieties of chop sticks, lacquered bowls, dishes, teapots, brush paintings, kimonos and other traditional arts and crafts. The Mother collected some issues of an art magazine called "Koka". Some of them have English translations of the articles and others are translated into French.

While living in Japan the Mother became friendly with Madame Kobayashi, the wife of a prominent doctor. The following is the beautiful description by Madame Kobayashi of their friendship.

"I loved her dearly. Have you seen those lovely wisteria* flowers trailing the roof of the Kasuga shrine at Nara? We call them hooji. My friend loved those flowers. She was one with them. She called herself Hoojiko when she thought of having a Japanese name...

"It was my great good fortune that, in this strange but explicable world, I should have met this jewel of my heart and this friend of my soul. The perfume of those two years, when we lived like twin roses on the same stalk, lingers like incense around the divine altar and sways serenely in the sanctuary of my mind."

Viewing the Srismriti Museum was an experience that remains profoundly etched in my memory.

* * *

*The Mother's significance for the wisteria flower is Poet's Ecstasy.

Mother with Madame Kobayashi in Kyoto, Japan,
around 1919

In closing I asked Sunanda to give me an assessment of her fifty years in the Ashram and what the Integral Yoga had done for her at her then age of sixty-six. This was her reply:

"I am here because I could not exist anywhere else. Mother has filled a void created in me in 1973 when she left her body by allowing me to see her presence in the subtle physical world that she shows to me now and then. On the days when I sincerely want to see her, she appears to me vividly. She allows my travel in the subtle physical regions on various levels. I also see and feel Sri Aurobindo more vividly since 1973 than ever before. The other world, the side beyond the curve feels very near. The psychic, the soul, the Atman, Paramatman exist in a shimmering, throbbing, scintillating light. There is no sense of separateness, no individuality. I could never tear myself from such an existence as I have here in the Ashram. How and why should I give it up?"

*   *   *

Two children's stories by Sunanda Poddar, written at about age twenty-two and taken from her books *Rainbow Lands* and *We Five and Other Tales*, follow.

Fairy Friends

After a very special dinner, they visited the library room in the princess's Garden Home.

It was a large room but divided into small areas. The bookcases were made with bamboo arranged in such a way that all the books had lots of breathing space. They were not cramped against each other.

There were bamboo step-ladders to reach the high shelves too.

Each small area had books classified according to various subjects like space, water, air, sky, animals, insects, trees, etc. and each section again had sub-divisions. For example the water section had seas, rivers, lakes, waterfalls, oceans as sub-divisions. And there were books and books.

There were tiny mini-books, there were huge tomes, there were sets bound in leather with gold embossed titles. Some volumes had covers of gold and silver engraved beautifully. There were talking books, musical books and books on flowers where you could smell the scent of each flower if you scratched them gently. And there were books printed on wood, leaves, bark, an cloth besides of course paper of many kinds.

It was indeed the best library of books they had ever seen.

At ten o'clock the huge clock glowed up with sparkling beams. The chime of ten was created with tinkling bells, ding-dong gongs, ringing ting-a-ling, trembling bars and thrilling drum beats.

"With the musical notes still fresh in our ears let us go to our rooms," Shekhar sir said softly.

"Oh, not so soon," several voices were heard.

"You have all had a long day," argued Mona's aunt.

"But this is a picnic!"

It was then decided that they could all have a little walk in the garden before going to bed.

"Look there, in that jasmine bush, there is a glow-worm,"

someone whispered.

"Yes, but there are more than one."

"One, two, three, four and two more there makes six and that little one seven!"

"Yes, there are seven of them!"

Virat pointed at the seven stars that make the group called Saptarishi.

They walked around the garden adding up other seven things and enjoyed the night breeze that carried, with its coolness, the fragrance of flowers and leaves.

And as if from nowhere rain drops were felt. Everyone had to hurry back to their rooms at last.

Mona and Bharat went straight to their windows to look for the glow-worms.

"They must have taken shelter just as we have," Bharat said.

"Yet the outside looks so fine at night" Mona said, as she gazed at the trees swaying in the wind that was gaining force slowly.

"I think we will have a storm tonight. Come, let us get into bed," Virat Uncle called them.

"If the storm comes, the rest of our picnic may not be such fun as it was today." Bharat was worried.

"But we shall have a rainbow in the sky when the sun comes out in the morning."

Mona jumped out of bed early. She woke up Bharat and both of them tiptoed out into the garden.

The rain and the wind had made their retreat. The clouds broke up and parts of pure, melting blue peeped out. The sun was restless to burst forth and paint the east with red, orange, yellow and gold. The colors poured a flood of glory over the earth.

Every flower and leaf shone, dripping with moisture, and started to breathe again. This was indeed a changed place.

"This feels like your land over the rainbow," Bharat whispered very, very softly.

"Yes, now the fairies and little people will come out to greet the sunlight." Mona's voice was even softer than a whisper.

And there were millions of glittering sun-filled sparks all around. Scarlet, white and blue, pink, red and violet, yellow and orange all tangled in utter confusion. The fairies were getting up and stretching their tender limbs and shaking their dainty wings and limp dresses. Little men dressed in green shirts and caps ran out of their leafy homes and hopped about and turned cartwheels. The fairies shook their wings dry and started flying around. But most of them went to rest among the flowers and leaves to receive the warmth of the morning sun.

But there was one little being left on the heap of bruised flower petals and broken leaves. It lay there absolutely still.

Mona picked it up tenderly. Now she was holding a fairy in her hand. She was a glowing, slender bundle. Careful not to crush or even press her tiny body, Mona held her most tenderly.

"Is she dead?" Bharat asked gently.

"No, she is so perfectly lovely she cannot be dead. Besides, I don't feel sad. So she must be alive though she is hurt," Mona explained.

She bent on this precious form and blew a whiff of light

air on her. There was a faint little thrill in the tiny form in her hand. An answering thrill of joy ran through Mona and Bharat. More softly, tenderly they both sent warm breaths to the hurt fairy. In a few more moments, Mona began to feel the smallest fluttering pulse of life throbbing faintly. In a few more minutes the fairy stirred more visibly and stretched her wings.

Now they saw. One of her wings had broken just near her shoulder and was holding on only by a silken thread to her body.

Oh God! what were they to do? How could they help her? How could they help to put right the wing?

They both looked around the garden. A large spider web was held up, in all its silvery glory, between two plants.

"Shall we take a thread from the web to repair the wings?" Bharat asked very quietly.

"Will it hold" Would it not do more damage?"

"Can we ask the dragon-fly to give us some broken wings from the ground?" Bharat wanted so much to help the fairy.

"To put a patch? No, I don't think it would take the weight. Our friend's wings are so very delicate".

"What then?" They were desperate, so keen to help."

When nothing else helps and there is no other way, we pray. Let us pray," Mona said.

So they just closed their eyes and called for help.

The sun warmed Mona's palm. The warmth and the heat felt good. The wind mildly blew over them. The gentle breeze shook the leaves above in the jasmine bush. The fragrances from the white star-like jasmine came and touched Mona's hand and the fairy's wings. The sunbeams and the scent-filled wind and the tiny drops of water enveloped them.

Everything was so peaceful. Feeling a slight movement in the fairy's wing, Mona opened her eyes. The prayer was still on their lips. It was delightful to watch the slow return of life to the wing.

The emerald green of the garden, the blue of the sky and the golden glow of the sun were healing their tiny friend.

"Oh look, she is standing up," Bharat noticed.

"Yes, she will soon fly away to her friends," Mona said, a little sadly.

Soon some other fairies came out from their flower-beds and leafy canopies.

They called the fairy in Mona's hand and danced in a circle around them.

After a while they took off, flying up above the trees.

"Look, they are flying in seven lines. Violet, Indigo, Blue, Green, Yellow, Orange and Red."

And there in the sky, the rainbow came out to receive them.

One Plant Many Flowers

In a small garden, on a plant in the corner there were lots of flowers all bursting out at a time to bloom. The playful breeze came and whistled and played hide and seek with the blossoms. He whispered to them the stories of distant lands and when he left, he carried with him their fragrance.

The breeze left.

The leaves and the flowers rustled no more. Calm peace

was everywhere. But in this quietness the flowers became restless.

They wanted to do something. The silence was too much to bear. They started wishing for something to happen.

A man came. He wanted to collect some flowers. But he would only take those that wanted to be taken. When he saw a flower not willing to be plucked, he left it alone.

The new flowers on this plant were very happy when the man came. At last something was happening. They wanted to be plucked, to be taken to new places.

The man plucked many, but there was one flower who turned its head away when he reached out to take it. The man understood at once. He let the flower be. The flowers already in his basket asked all at once "Why don't you come? We will be able to do so much. We will go to so many places."

But that flower was not willing to go.

The man took the other flowers. Only one flower remained on the plant. Once again there was peace.

After some time the breeze came back to play with the flowers. Most of the flowers were gone. He was shocked. "Where have they all gone?"

"To different places." the remaining flower replied.

"But why?"

"They wanted to do something. It was too quiet here."

"Oh! and I came to take a little more of their lovely fragrance." The breeze looked sadly at the flower.

But the flower smiled beautifully and with that smile a huge amount of fragrance poured out. The breeze was so happy, it started dancing around this flower. It ruffled the petals and the flower gave out more and more of its lovely scent.

Then the breeze took some of this scent and left.

The flower became quiet once more.

It grew up all alone.

Some more time passed.

The breeze came once again to the garden. The lone flower was fading its colors. The petals were drooping. The breeze was very sad. It was afraid to go near the flower. But the flower smiled and called him near.

"No, if I come near, you will lose your petals," the breeze said.

"In any case I am going to fall. Please come."

The breeze went near very gently. The flower swayed with joy in the breeze and fell. It lay on the ground.

The breeze took the last fragrance of the flower and left.

Now, he wanted to go and see where the rest of the flowers from that plant were and what they had done. He was sure he would recognize them because he had known their fragrance.

So he went in search of the flowers. He felt the fragrance of those flowers in all directions. A whiff from the left and from the right. A mild smell pulled him in front while a strong perfume came from the back. Some of it was on the ground, some of it in the air. He was really happy and moved fast to meet these flowers spread in all directions.

One by one he visited them.

All of them had done their various works and were fading away now. They all smiled at him as he went near them. They told him what they had done.

One flower had sat beautifully in the long hair of a lady who was getting married. One had gone to the hospital to cheer up a sick child. One had decorated a vase in a huge drawing room. One was woven in a garland for a victorious hero. One had been given as a gift with a silent message and was now resting between the pages of a book lovingly looked at from time to time. One had been offered to God at the temple. One had found its way to a student's table and had made the student learn all about the plants, the petals, the pollen, the leaves, the branches, the roots.

Collecting all these stories of the flowers, the breeze went back to the garden. He wanted to tell the one flower in the garden all that he had seen. He went near the plant and saw there a fading flower.

He looked and he searched. At last he saw a very tiny new plant that had just begun to grow.

From many instances I have come to know that my face is like a mirror showing each one the images of his/her own internal condition.

                                        The Mother

Richard Pearson

Richard Pearson

*(Teacher, Botanist, Captain and Editor of
'Flowers and Their Messages')*

Richard Pearson was just eleven years old when he first came
to the Sri Aurobindo Ashram with his English father in 1946,
after the close of World War II. He was born in the north of
England on November 1, 1934 in a town called Shepley in
Yorkshire. The town was thus named for its reputation of
being sheep country. As a child Richard was very close to
nature and animals and used to play in the grassy fields where
wild flowers bloomed and goats, sheep and other animals
grazed. His grandparents were of Russian Jewish heritage
and had left Russia for England. His father was born and
educated in England.

Both parents were nurses. Neither parent was keen on religion but Richard joined the local church choir. He remem-
bers the pastor saying that if they had any questions about
God, they could write and ask him. Richard did so and was
not satisfied with the answers. He thought he would write
about God! Later, when he was in the Ashram, he showed his
childhood writings to the Mother and she helped him with
spellings and said, "As you grow older your ideas about God
will also change." Richard said he was a rather austere, shy
young boy and somewhat fanatical about being morally correct.

When Richard was ten years old his father joined the Royal

Army Medical Corps as a nurse, and he saw very little of him after that time until the war ended. Richard's mother was left to care for the two children on her own. Reacting to some changes in his family life, Richard said he became a rather difficult child. During this period he was sent to live with other families and could not understand why he was always moving around constantly. He was unhappy without his mother and having to stay with so many strangers.

His father had been posted in India and wrote to Richard's mother that he wanted to settle in India when the war was over. He asked if they would like to come and live there. Remembering the jungle and wild animal stories he had read about, Richard said, "It's a great idea!"

Ultimately his mother took him to stay in a boarding school in Somerset "far from anywhere", he said. It was a boys' school and the headmistress was a terror. They were all underfed and lived in very trying conditions. Richard became a kind of mentor and counselor to the other boys and answered their questions to their satisfaction. Although he was alone and without family he said he never really felt alone. He felt that "somebody" or "something" was always with him; a Presence that he could feel. He used to lie in the wheat fields alone in the evenings looking up at the sky. On one of these evenings he had a very profound and concrete experience of the infinity of the universe and of the limitlessness of the sky. The more he would gaze the more limitless was his vision.

How did you eventually come to the Ashram to live?

My father was a reader of philosophy. He collected books on spirituality and philosophy. He had plenty of free time in India and read Sri Ramakrishna and Sri Ramana Maharshi. Soon he discovered Sri Aurobindo's *The Life Divine*. While in Calcutta, he went to the Sri Aurobindo Bhavan and met Rajen-da and Madan-da, who settled later in the Ashram. They encouraged him to seek permission to visit Sri Aurobindo Ashram. So on August 15, 1943 he had his first darshan of Sri Aurobindo and was completely taken in. I could not leave London until the war was over. By October of that year I left boarding school and stayed with my Mother's family for a time. Afterwards, I went to London to live with Norman Dowsett's family. [Norman Dowsett was a teacher in the Ashram school for many years.] My father had made an acquaintance with Norman Dowsett who was, at that time, in the Royal Air Force. I lived with them for four months and went to school in London. Later, I travelled with them to India by ship. We arrived in India on February 21, 1946. My father came to receive me at the port in Bombay. It was toward the end of the British rule and there was a "Quit India" movement at that time to get all the British out of India. We had to leave Bombay very quickly. We travelled two days together by train destined for Madras. We took another train for Pondicherry. On the train, my father took out his wallet and showed me photos of Mother and Sri Aurobindo and said, "We are going to see these two great people." I felt mystified by it. We went straight to Leena Dowsett's house. On arrival a message came to us, given to them by the Mother, that we were to see her after breakfast!

Could you describe that meeting with the Mother and your impressions?

We went with Udar, Norman and Leena and their children to Pavitra's room. My father said, "Fold your hands and say, 'Bonjour douce Mère'. If she touches you, you can touch her feet." I was just this shy little boy from England. Suddenly a dog came charging into the room. This was the Mother's dog named "Goldie". I was so fond of animals but this took me completely by surprise. Then, the dog left the room just as quickly as it had entered. At that moment, the Mother came in. It felt as though a strong gust of wind had swept into the room because there was such vitality in her presence. She said "Good morning, everybody" and shook each one's hand in a true English way. Everything happened so fast that I forgot all that I was supposed to say. She began to ask questions about our journey and if everything was all right.

Do you have any other impressions of the Mother?

One strong impression that I have of the Mother was that she was always dashing forward. One occasion that I remember when she showed this quality was in the playground during one of her Wednesday night talks. She had given a "bang" to our laziness as no one was asking questions. She was in a warrior mood. She marched out with such determination as if to show us how one is to move forward. The second instance was around 1956 during a rehearsal of the play "The Spiritual Destiny of India", in the Ashram school.

The Mother had taken a keen interest in the play and had given her directions for the smallest details. She was talking to the organizers and said, "And what shall we do next year?" That play had not yet taken place and the Mother was already planning ahead. This power of the Shakti was truly impressive to me.

When did you begin classes in the Ashram school? What was your life like in those early days?

I began school the very next day after meeting the Mother. I did not speak French so I had to learn. Later, it became such a fascination (because the Mother spoke to us in French) that I picked on anybody who could speak French well in order to better learn how to speak the language. Sunil-da became my teacher and later my mentor. He was very important to me and my intellectual growth and development. He taught me math, astronomy and botany. I left the Dowsetts' home within a few days and went to stay with Udar's family and took my meals with them. They taught me how to wear a dhoti. (My father had returned to Madras where he was still waiting for final clearance from the army.) There I met Ambu who became my model. I wanted to be strong like him and I learned asanas from him. He taught me how to wash my clothes, to dress like an Indian and to take care of things. I made friends with Gauri's dog, "Spotted Beauty", a Dalmatian. They also had a donkey named "Baudet". Udar had purchased it for the Mother and kept it in his garden. I asked Mother if I could look after it and she gave permission. Gauri was my friend but I did not have the

time or take the time to make other friendships. I spent a
great deal of time on their terrace looking out on the sea and
I began to write again. I began to see everything turning
itself to the Divine; the waves, the clouds. Everything gave
me the sense of self-giving and offering of itself to the Divine. I used to sit quietly and receive these impressions.
Since I was so shy I preferred to stay by myself. [The following is an example of Richard's childhood writings that
was shown to the Mother.]

By the sea

"We often watch the sea rushing towards land with its high
waves towering up. As they reach the shore, these waves
come down from their heights and roll up the beach in a thin
layer of white foam.

"The waves trying to reach the shore are like people trying to find the Divine.

"Some waves are big and have a lot of foam. They get
bigger as they come nearer the shore. They are just like the
rich people with a lot of money who are trying to get rid of
their riches to reach the Divine, but He is putting them through
a test — the more they give, the more they get.

"There are big waves and small waves, but it is all sea.
And there are rich men and poor men, but they are all the
Divine's children seeking their Divine Mother.

"As they come nearer, the waves all come together, and
joyfully they rush on to the beach. People coming near to the
Divine collect together. They bend down and all becomes
love for the Divine."

Will you please share your experience of the first darshan with Sri Aurobindo?

In the early days there was no line except from the Meditation Hall. Everyone sat in the courtyard. We had a three-day holiday from school; the day before darshan, darshan day and the day after, which was called Garland Day. It felt as though one walked in some other world. We entered the darshan room and it felt like a cool, dense forest, intense and quiet. Although I was so short and there were tall people in front of me and I couldn't see, I could feel a solid peace — something very solid... a force, a light, intangible but inexpressible. Even though they sat in the anteroom one had a sense of being in the same room with Mother and Sri Aurobindo. Sri Aurobindo for me, as a child, was like viewing a mountain. He was so majestic. When I was still quite young I used to wonder what he was doing in his room all day and why we only saw him four times a year. The Mother seemed like a Queen when she sat next to Sri Aurobindo. Sri Aurobindo was truly regal. His presence was felt even before standing in front of him. There was a great coolness in the room. The very first time I entered the Ashram I could feel this coolness and peace in the atmosphere. To this very day when I am in a state of deep quietude, I can still feel this atmosphere of Sri Aurobindo's darshan very strongly. Sri Aurobindo looked austere and impassive. The Mother was radiant and smiling! There were some darshan days when the Mother would be in a trance. Sri Aurobindo would be smiling and gracious. One felt a warmth and sweetness from him.

Darshan days were quite different from other days when one met with the Mother. They were a much more powerful experience. Mother said darshan is the culmination or the fulfillment of a great deal of work that had been done. One had to prepare for the darshan within oneself to receive the blessing. Mother said, "Preparation in oneself is what makes darshan so special."

What did you do after you finished your courses in the Ashram school?

I had asked Mother if I should take my higher courses in England. She wrote back:

"I intended to let you go for your studies in England without telling you anything about it, because each one must be free to follow the path he has chosen. But after what you have written I feel compelled to write to you.

"No doubt from the exterior point of view, you will find in England all that you want for learning what human beings generally call knowledge, but from the point of view of Truth and Consciousness, you can find nowhere the atmosphere in which you are living here. Elsewhere you can meet with a religious or a philosophic spirit, but true spirituality, direct contact with the Divine, constant aspiration to realise Him in life, mind and action are in the world realised only by scattered individuals and not as a living fact behind any university teaching however advanced it may be.

"Physically, as far as you are concerned, there will be a great risk of drifting away from the experience you have realized and then you cannot know what will happen to you. That is all I wanted to say — now it is left to you to choose and decide."

Of course, I did not go. The Mother then said I could study botany in the Ashram library and I received special permission from Medhananda to do so. Mother asked me to take on teaching an English class in the school while I was studying. At the age of 18, I was only slightly older than the students that I was teaching. When the new lab opened, Mother told me to work there. This was my first training in physical work done for the Mother. I labelled bottles, packets, lab equipment and chemicals. Then a separate room was given for natural history items such as seeds, feathers and dried fruits of plants and trees, stones and even an elephant's head! I was given permission to keep and attend to wounded animals; snakes, crows, squirrels, etc. When Mother received pressed flowers and other plants, etc., she would send them to me to keep carefully. Mother would write and give me guidelines about so many things. Particularly about teaching and outings. I used to take the children on nature outings and would go on nature outings with Sunil-da.

I hear that you received the "Prix d'Honneur" from the Mother. Can you tell us something about it?

Well, from 1954 the Mother had started to give a special award of recognition, called "Prix d'Honneur" to a student who showed exceptional qualities in all the activities and branches of education and whose conduct conformed to the ideal of the Ashram from all points of view. It was in 1955 that the Mother chose this honor for me.

Did you ever live with your father?

I lived with Udar's family for a few months until my father arrived, after being released from the army. The Mother gave him a room and I stayed with him until 1956 at which time he left. He got several schools started on the lines of the Mother and Sri Aurobindo; one in Bhagalpur, one at the Delhi Ashram and one in Bangalore. It was in 1962 that he invited me to help him as a teacher in Bangalore.

Did you go?

I asked the Mother. She replied to me in strong and touching words. She said, "Richard, my dear child: I have absolutely no intention of letting you leave from here — we have need of you and your excellent work. I consider you like my son and I have great confidence in your future from the point of view of yoga. With my blessings."

Tell me about your connection with physical education and how you became a captain?

In the very beginning I was not so interested in games and sports but I did love gymnastics and swimming. We also had more of boxing than I enjoyed, since Biren Chandra, our captain and leader, was a well-known boxer.

Later, when the Mother sat and watched the strong men,

boys and a couple of girls doing strengthening exercises after group was over, I used to practise roller-balancing in a corner by myself. Even later, our captain gathered together a select group to study, reflect and discuss the means of applying Mother's and Sri Aurobindo's teachings in our life and activities both individually and collectively.

When my name was suggested for taking group as a captain the Mother refused to accept it. She told me that I should not have to run from one activity to another. "Work done well is work done quietly," she added. When the Captains' Group was formed in 1963, however, it was the Mother who then accepted my joining. I was chosen to address the prayer to her in the playground on the occasion of wearing our new uniform (24 April 1963).

How did you meet Kailas and in what way did the Mother encourage your relationship?

Our meeting came at a time when I had overworked myself. I had no servant and was teaching and doing the lab work. I wanted to take a beehive from a tree trunk and set about to do this on my own and I was stung. One sting became septic and a stinger remained in one little finger. I had to go to the nursing home and Dr. Sanyal operated to remove the stinger. After this he went to New York for his own operation for Parkinson's Disease and Kailas met him while there. He told her when she was ready to come to the Ashram he would arrange for a place for her to stay. The nurse who looked after me was Janina, the artist. She brought me back to life as I was in a critical stage. I had no stamina and was very

Kailas and Anie, Ashram Theatre, 1968

Kailas and Richard – Matagiri, New York, 1999

weak and thin. Mother gave Janina the Force for this work. She showed me that the dark side of oneself is also one's self and has to be accepted and offered to the Mother. Janina passed away on her birthday, July 17, 1964.

Kailas arrived August 14, 1964. She was brought to the nursing home as there was no vacancy anywhere in the Ashram. I was thirty years old at that time. Kailas taught me how to be open with myself. I did not have many friends and didn't know how to make social contact. I went with Kailas to see the Mother on her birthday, June 11, 1965. Mother gave several large books to Kailas and turned to me and said, "Aren't you a gentleman?" She meant that I should have thought of helping Kailas with the books, but I was so shy. I was a different person before Kailas arrived. I was always resisting everything and reluctant to show my feelings. I would not even stop to take tea. Mona Pinto used to say about me, "This boy never had a mother!"

Kailas would ask, "Is there anything you would like to discuss?" I wasn't accustomed to that kind of interaction, but began to find the value of sharing my thoughts and feelings with others. During that period the Mother sent us a copy of *Sri Aurobindo or the Adventure of Consciousness* and asked us to read it together. This drew us closer together and we began to have fixed times for meditation and to share our meals. Kailas was so free, full of vitality and exuberance that I began to change from a shy person to a sociable, joyous one.

Kailas and I had two things in common: a love of beauty and a love of flowers. She knew their significances. She had started a sort of communion with the Mother through flowers which lasted for over four years. She started it by sending a dinner-size dish filled with "purity" (jasmine) with a lotus-shaped small vase in the center, holding a rose of "Surrender", both of which indicated her aspiration. The Mother took them herself and filled her dish with flowers of "Divine Grace". This went on for as long as the "Divine Grace" was blooming. I watched this with great interest. The Mother then changed the flowers to the "Supramental Psychological Perfection", again as long as they were in season, with the "Supramental Consciousness" in the center. Then the dish would come back with flowers of "Perfect Radiating Purity", "Purity in Action" and so on. The central flowers could change to the "Supramental Sun" or anything connected with the Supramental or Sachchidananda. The Mother would arrange these flowers herself. After some time, I too started, when given permission, to send flowers for the Mother. The last flowers the Mother sent to me were a garland of "Devotion". I used to press all the flowers sent to us. We would send flowers covered with a beautiful cloth. In the Indian tradition, when flowers are given to the guru, they should not be seen, touched nor smelled by anyone else.

Mother said, "When I give them [flowers] I give you states of consciousness." [*Flowers and their Messages IX*]

> *When did the flower work begin and the work on the book* Flowers and Their Messages?

I was always touched by the array of flowers arranged in trays when we went one by one to see the Mother. Mother would give us a flower and look deeply into our eyes, so very deep. I would take the flower straight home and keep it in a bottle or vase and would keep it fresh for as long as possible. ["Answering with the flower's answer to the sun, they gave themselves to her and asked no more." *Savitri*, Book IV, Canto 2.]

From the beginning when I saw the book by Lizelle Raymond, a French woman living in the Ashram, who wrote *Le Rôle de Fleurs*, published in 1953, I found the introduction to be a masterpiece. It was about how flowers were offered to the Mother and how the Mother gave her blessings through flowers. "There are three ways of blessing of the Mother: by sight, by touch and through flowers. And it is through flowers that her blessing is most effective," Sri Aurobindo is reported to have written. I was very touched by the book. All the flowers were in order according to the French names given. When I saw it I found some mistakes in the botanical names and in the significances. I wrote to the Mother asking if I could work on a flower book that would contain all the names Mother had given. Mother said "Yes, this could be done." This development began the new classification in 1957, but was not completed until 1973. During this work, Pavitra sent messages to the Mother for me. He was another of my mentors. When I went to his room, as soon as I entered, I would feel that I was in the Mother's room, so strong was her Force. In his presence I would feel the presence of the Mother. [Pavitra, a Frenchman, whose European name was P.B. Saint-Hilaire, was a highly skilled scientist and engineer. He was head of the Ashram school and secretary to the Mother. Pavitra's name, given by Sri Aurobindo, means "the pure".]

When Auroville was inaugurated and the idea for the twelve gardens was being worked out with Roger, Mother called me to bring as many hibiscus flowers as possible to Auroville. I went every Tuesday. At the first meeting with Mother she explained that she wanted to choose a hibiscus flower for each of the twelve gardens. The first day she chose "Supramental Consciousness" for the Garden of Consciousness. "It is so luminous," she remarked. Richard Eggenberger (named Narad by the Mother) helped me in bringing the flowers. The work on the flowers began with great vigor in the first gardens of Auroville when Narad started the nursery for Matrimandir Gardens in 1969. He collected many varieties and beautifully built up the gardens.

Hibiscus flowers would come from the nursery for the Mother and would be left at the Ashram reception. Kailas and I would go and, if possible, paint these flowers before they went upstairs. Mother first called "Godhead" the Auroville flower, but then changed it to "Beauty of Supramental Love". She told me that this flower was similar to the rich, red color of Auroville soil. Many hibiscus were given names for Auroville: "The Success of Auroville", "The Firmness of Auroville", "The Concentration of Auroville", etc. Later, she changed the word Auroville to "New Creation".

The biggest gift from the Mother for the work with flowers were the commentaries she gave on the flowers. The Mother would work on about five flowers a day at a fixed time. This was checked the following day by Tara. These commentaries done in 1970 and 1971 were for the "flower book" which was still in progress. When they were translated by Tehmi into English, Narad came in the evenings, all the way from Auroville, to help with the botanical and common names and descriptions of the flowers and the plants for *Flowers and Their Messages*. Since Mother used flowers as a help for our spiritual progress, Kailas felt that relevant quotations from the writings of the Mother and Sri Aurobindo would help the reader, so she chose appropriate passages. Lyn Miller did the line drawings. At later stages I would go to the press to check certain details in the hand-set final proofs. The book was one of the early publications from Auropress.

> *Can you further share any stories about the Mother, more on your work for her or special anecdotes that you remember?*

The Mother was so fond of flowers, according to Jyotin-da, that in the early days, before the Ashram had gardens, to him the old saying "beg, borrow or steal" was the method used to procure flowers for the Mother for distribution. So, with hurricane lantern, stick and basket in hand and a pair of nimble legs to climb over walls, our would-be gardeners went out by night or very early morning. Perhaps in those days of rigorous sadhana, when you would not go for a walk or to visit another sadhak without the Mother's express permission, the end justified the means! But when during one such "sortie" a sadhak, who was not quick enough to jump the fence, was caught and even put behind bars for the offence, the Mother decided it was time to develop gardens and gardening. One of the first gardens, Maret Garden, was called "Atal's Garden" by the sadhaks, for Atal, the very same person who went to jail, was put in charge!

Those were the days when houses or gardens could be haunted by spirits up to some mischief, so dear Atal-da had to deal, himself, with not-so-pleasant intruders!

After a few years the townspeople too, really came to know of the Mother's magical ways of forcing "Matter to express the Spirit".

Once the Mother had decided that flowers would be grown in our gardens, she encouraged gardeners to try out all sorts of new varieties of flowers and vegetables. When a flower and vegetable show was arranged at the local botanical garden in Pondicherry, the flowers and plants displayed by the Ashram created an overwhelming presence of beauty and joy and peace: the beauty and bliss of the Divine Mother's Grace! ["Flowers bring with them the smile of the Divine" — from *Prayers and Meditations*.]

Many were the stories Jyotin-da, another sadhak, would tell. This is one that had baffled him when he tried to fathom the Mother's ways with her children. He told me of a flower I had not seen though I knew the tree. It was "Jerusalem Thorn" (Parkinsonia aculeata). He had taken it several times to the Mother when he saw it bloom, but she had not given it any significance. Others had tried asking her but in vain. It was during the very early days of Auroville and there was a young girl in her teens who had come to the Mother on her birthday. She brought these flowers with their feathery leaves to Mother. Mother smiled as she took the flowers and exclaimed, "Oh, this is Lightness!" The girl, with lovely blonde hair flowing over her shoulders, was studying to be a ballet dancer! Pavitra once asked me, when I was enthusiastically

trying to persuade him to ask the Mother about a particular
significance: "Do you think the Mother gives the name for
the flowers, or for us?" At that moment I truly believed she
gave names only to the flowers, but after this and other such
experiences, I am convinced that it is both terrestrial and an
individual gift of the Divine Mother.

With the children who arrived with their parents after 1939,
little by little a new energy was present in the Ashram and
one of the first things the Mother did was to use the French
name for the flowers when talking with the children. By 1943,
when the school officially opened, French became the language of instruction, as Mother would speak in French. The
greetings of "Bonjour!" and "Bonne Fête!" have defied time
and space and even now form that beautiful bond that unites
us all with her. Also, the Mother encouraged all forms of art
and handiwork — embroidery, painting, carpentry, leather
work — all means of expressing beauty by consecrated service and work, obliging matter to obey the spirit! The Ashram
artists were only a handful in those days; Anilbaran, Jayantilal,
Krishnalal, Sanjiban, etc. They painted as their offering to
her. Though interested in land or seascapes, they also painted
flowers for the Mother to name and she kept these paintings
in Pavitra's room until they were later moved to The Studio.

> *How did you feel when you went to the Mother on your*
> *birthday?*

The following quotation from *Prayers and Meditations*
would best describe what we felt when the Mother gave
flowers for our birthday, the most special day, individually

speaking, of the year. We saw her several times on that day and each time we would receive a special bouquet or garland and her special flower, her smile and her presence.

"Each time that a heart leaps at the touch of Thy divine breath, a little more beauty seems to be born upon the Earth, the air is embalmed with a sweet perfume, all becomes more friendly....

"At these blessed hours all earth sings a hymn of gladness, the grasses shudder with pleasure, the air is vibrant with light, the trees lift towards heaven their most ardent prayer, the chant of the birds becomes a canticle, the waves of the sea billow with love, the smile of the children tells of the infinite and the souls of men appear in their eyes." [*Prayers and Meditations*, March 31, 1917.]

*   *   *

Richard and Kailas continue to offer their lives in service to the Mother. They are well known and loved in the United States and have visited many centers giving talks and beautiful slide presentations on *Flowers and Their Messages*. They live in the Ashram but visit Auroville frequently. They receive and assist visitors and newcomers and both have given talks at the Savitri Bhavan in Auroville, participating in the series of intimate sharings entitled: "Remembering the Mother".

Be conscious first of thyself within,
then think and act.

Sri Aurobindo

Pain is the hand of Nature
sculpturing men to greatness...

Sri Aurobindo

Jhumur Bhattacharya

Jhumur Bhattacharya

(*Teacher in the Sri Aurobindo International Centre of Education, actress in Sri Aurobindo's plays and dancer*)

Jhumur is one of the true swans of the Ashram. Tall, statuesque, regal and elegant she gracefully moves about the Ashram compound in beautifully hand-painted saris and most of the time she carries with her lovely and colorful parasols that protect her fair skin from the scorching tropical sun.

She, her cousin Chum and her elderly aunt, Minnie-di are the last three of one of the Ashram's original families who still reside in the "Art House", their large French-style colonial residence on Jawaharlal Nehru Street in Pondicherry. Jhumur graciously welcomed me into her home on each day of the interviews and her regal bearing and inner and outer beauty are indications of a life lived in pursuit of higher values and spiritual goals. Her purity of purpose became more and more evident to me as the interviews proceeded. She was born in Calcutta on November 27, 1939. Her great-aunt, her paternal grandmother's sister, was one of the first disciples of Sri Aurobindo in West Bengal. The aunt, Indubala Banerji, immediately recognized Sri Aurobindo as her guru and he gave her a very specific work. She had begun to read Sri Aurobindo's early writings, came into contact with him and he asked her to start a center just outside Calcutta. Many who were followers at that time later became the first

ashramites. Among them were Noren Das Gupta, Manoj Das
Gupta's father and Rajani Palit, Romen's father, and some
of Jhumur's family members. They were required to live in
the center and work together as a spiritual family in order to
prepare themselves for life in the Ashram when Sri Aurobindo
would declare them sufficiently ready for this next step. They
were not permitted to go to the Ashram for darshan until Sri
Aurobindo had said yes. Her father told her that his family
used to say prayers daily to Sri Aurobindo. They were all
worshippers of Shakti Force and always worshipped together
as a family. The entire village came to their home for Kali
puja.

The Bhattacharya family is descended from the highest
caste of Brahmin priests. About seven generations before her
grandfather's time they had been priests to the royal family
of Assam (in those times known as Kamrup). Their story goes
back to the original ruler who was not of Hindu or Aryan
origin, but, rather, a Mongol. Jhumur was not quite certain of
all the exact details of the legend because her grandfather
and father are no longer alive to verify certain facts, but she
has given the story to me to the best of her memory. The
ruler had a dream in which he saw a Brahmin sadhu giving
diksha (a blessing or initiation). In the dream he saw the sadhu
standing by the waters of the Ganges, facing a particular direction and holding a stone. The king asked his ministers to
go there and search for this sadhu and to bring him back to
the palace in Assam. This was Jhumur's ancestor. He was
found and brought to the king where he converted him to
Hinduism and initiated him into a new path of spiritual practice. From that time to some time in the 1800s no one in the

family worked. The priests of the family performed all rites for the king and his successors such as weddings, coronations, funerals, pujas (religious rituals) and the king and subsequent rulers gave the family jewels, silks, tea, land and all the monies from the growing of crops on the land went to the family members.

The original stone was in the family's keeping for many generations to come. It was always the eldest son in the family who presided over all the religious ceremonies and who was the keeper of the sacred stone. A special temple was built to house the stone and only the eldest son was allowed to enter the temple and attend to its safety. Seers had predicted that so long as the stone remained within the family unit the family would flourish. Then family members began to disperse and to go off elsewhere to study law, medicine and pursue other careers. Jhumur's grandfather had become a doctor. Soon there were no family members qualified to preside as priests in the home and none to take care of the stone. Eventually, the remaining family members had to hire outside priests to come to their home to perform puja. These priests soon began to take the stone with them to their homes and then the Bhattacharya family house completely broke up. Ultimately refugees began to pour into West Bengal from East Bengal and the land now belongs to the government and is used partly for agriculture, partly for housing.

Word was sent to Sri Aurobindo when Jhumur's parents married in 1936 after which special blessings came to them for their marriage directly from Sri Aurobindo. So deep was their devotion that they automatically accepted the divinity of Sri Aurobindo without question.

In 1937, a year after their marriage, Millie-di, Jhumur's mother, gave birth to a baby boy who was born with hydrocephalus. Millie-di suffered blood poisoning and after childbirth almost died. Sunil Bhattacharya, Jhumur's uncle and the well-known composer and musician in the Ashram, was also a gifted astrologer. Jhumur said that the baby was a beautiful child and that Sunil had said he had exceptional markings on his hands; all the markings of a Rishi. Millie-di wrote to the Mother almost every day praying to her and asking her to take the child. He was called Khoka, which means simply "Little Boy" in Bengali. Millie-di used to sit and hold him in her arms and rock him. On November 24, 1939 — she was expecting Jhumur at that time, Millie-di was sitting in meditation in observance of Sri Aurobindo's Siddhi day when suddenly and quietly the little boy passed away. Jhumur was born three days later.

When did your family permanently settle in Pondicherry?

When my mother and I moved to Pondicherry it was 1942 and I was just three years old. Our family often visited Pondicherry. Nolini had also lived in the Calcutta center and his sons as well. His sons had also lived in our house and all our correspondence to the Mother and Sri Aurobindo went through Nolini. At that time my father was still in the British Army and stationed in the Middle East. He was a strong man and loved to travel. He also took part in various maneuvers of bombing attacks and was trained for the army in Maharashtra and Jaipur. My father joined us in the

Jhumur in her room at Art House, Dec. 2002

Jhumur and Millie-di at Art House, 2001

Ashram after World War II was over.

What was life like in the Ashram in those early days?

Well, in those days children under age four were not allowed to be in the presence of Mother and Sri Aurobindo and had to stand back two blocks away near the French Institute. The pressure was too strong for small children. Slowly and gradually children were allowed to come closer. As children we used to feel badly that we could not go to the Ashram main building. I remember sidling inside where the bulletin board is kept where we were not allowed. Eventually, someone told the Mother that the children were not happy because we were not able to go up and see her. Then she said we could come to her on the 15th of every month. We went by ourselves to the Mother. It was a very special time. She used to organize children's games for us around her apartment and sing to us. This went on until after age four. She would ask us what we had studied, about any poems we had learned. I had learned a poem about a tiger which I recited to Mother. Mother helped me with the poem. The Mother became "excited" and told me, "You must feel the power of the tiger." When I grew older I was allowed to visit Mother every day. The Mother was very busy overseeing every department of the Ashram. Some of us (Tara Jauhar, Gauri Pinto and others) would go up at mid-day after school and wait at the top of the staircase. She evolved games that we played with her as she wanted us to develop our memory and impressions. There were occult powers in precious stones (amethyst, sapphire, ruby) and she made up cards explaining the various meaning of the stones. The same game was devised for learning the spiritual meanings and significance of flowers and plants. From these games I learned how to read very well.

As I grew older, especially towards the end before Mother left her body, I would go to her and automatically I would feel the sense of belonging to her only and that nothing else counted or mattered. She would look deeply into my being with her eyes wide open. It was as though I had become immersed in the ocean and was drowning. I was eleven years old when Sri Aurobindo left his body. The Mother said, "Now I must teach you something about sadhana. Have you read *Prayers and Meditation?*" She gave each of us a copy signed by her and she said, "Every Wednesday after March Past, gymnastics, concentration and distribution of sweets and prasad, I will teach a class." Thus on Wednesday nights she began the talks that were later published as *Questions and Answers*. Everyone joined in. She taught us young people the deeper meaning of yoga and sadhana gradually and slowly.

Can you speak to me about your impressions of Sri Aurobindo. What do you remember ?

Sri Aurobindo was a magnificent sight. He was golden colored and looked the embodiment of majesty and grandeur. We saw the Mother every day but only saw Sri Aurobindo four times each year. I never saw him stand up but his grandeur seemed to me, at so young an age, to be a combination of all the kings of the world in one form! I always tried to get a good look at him before standing before him for darshan. I just immediately knew from within that he

was the Absolute in human form. There was no talking, no
words, only the offering of garlands to him.

*I know that you performed in many of Sri Aurobindo's
plays in the Ashram school and theatre. I saw you in
many performances. How did this expression begin for
you?*

By the time I was eight years old in 1947 I loved to recite.
The Mother said, "I will teach you some lines from the poem
'Jeanne d'Arc'." The lines were so beautiful. I did not perform at that time, but Mother said, "It will happen at another time." Years later in 1984 Cristof (a member of the
famous Pitoev family of French actors) wrote a play about
Jeanne d'Arc who died at age nineteen. I was asked to play
the lead. I said, "I can't now because my father is ill and in
the nursing home so I am not free. Please ask someone else."
Cristof said, "If it is not you, it won't be done!" A few
months later my father recovered and Cristof said, "Now
will you do it?" Then I remembered Mother's words and
said "Yes". Acting gave me so many experiences. I could
plunge into the innermost depths of my being and it put
me in touch with my psychic being. Mother said if you perform anything written by Sri Aurobindo, he, too, will always be there. All of my performances were an offering to
them. The audience was not important to me. Mother said
acting is not for show, never should it be, but rather it is for
the growth of one's consciousness. My mother created all
the costumes. Everything was organized by the Mother and
she would come to the "Art House" to make suggestions

and changes where they were needed.

In about 1960 the Government of India sent a commission to visit our Centre of Education and to observe the Ashram. Pavitra suggested that we put on a performance with music in the theatre in English and in French. He choose a long prayer from Mother's *Prayers and Meditations* for me to recite (March 31,1917) with Srimoy (another member of the Pitoev family of actors). Srimoy had such a very dramatic delivery that I did not particularly like and she insisted that I recite it in the way she was reciting. Three days before the performance I lost my voice. I went to Pavitra but could not speak. I said, "You must choose someone else." Pavitra went to Mother's apartment and the Mother said, "Is Jhumur outside?" I went in and Mother said,"Give me the book." Mother read it once and said, "You listen." The second time she said, "You listen. Now you must keep absolutely quiet, do not speak for three days, only eat and drink. Don't rehearse and stay quiet until you go on stage." When I opened my mouth during performance it was very clear to me that Mother, herself, was speaking through me.

Performing was so helpful for my sadhana. I would make a personal prayer to Sri Aurobindo and call to him strongly. My prayer was, "I pray that I do this in the way in which you would want me to do it." His help did come. I felt his Force. From December 1, 1958 Mother no longer came physically to the theatre, but she said, "Every year on December 1, you can be sure that I shall be present in the theatre during *Savitri* presentation." Now and then I do see her.

What plays of Sri Aurobindo did you take part in?

Well, there was *Vasavadutta, Rodogune, Perseus the Deliverer, Vikramorvasie (The Hero and The Nymph)* to name a few and of course *Savitri*.

What other guidance did Mother give to you for your sadhana?

I remember going to her and telling her that I just didn't want to continue to grow taller and taller and taller! My father's family were very tall. I said to Mother, "I don't want to be so tall anymore. I am always put with the boys and it is not fashionable to be so tall. Mother, please let me stop growing."

"Why?", she said, "It is nice to be tall. To grow tall is a sign of the body's aspiration for the Divine." After she spoke those words I was never again bothered by my height.

What is the atmosphere of the Ashram like for you since Mother and Sri Aurobindo are no longer in a physical form?

Now one has to concentrate more inwardly to find them. Sometimes it is possible to come almost physically into contact with them. I see them sometimes on the subtle physical planes. One year, sometime in the 1990s, I saw Mother sitting and smiling in the Ashram theatre. During the 50th anniversary celebration of the playground, I was going to Sri Aurobindo's room in playground uniform and I was facing Mother's balcony. Suddenly, I saw her come out dressed all in white and for a moment I forgot that she was not actu-

ally physically there. In the August 1995 Bulletin of Sri
Aurobindo International Centre of Education, one of the
Ashram photographers had taken a photo of Mother's balcony and it shows Mother standing there, in kitty cap, in a
subtle physical form! So you see, she is still with us and
continues to show us that she is there in our midst, from
time to time. Sometimes I even smell Mother's perfume. It
is not an actual fragrance, but comes from the subtle realms.
It is also the same with Sri Aurobindo that I smell a subtle
fragrance, then I know that they are both present.

In 1972, a year before Mother left her body, on a visit to
her she said to me in French, "On ne se quitte pas" ("I will
never leave you"). On another occasion she also said to me
in French, "Ces mains, je les connais!" ("I know these
hands").

What changes do you see taking place in the Ashram?

We must be true to what Mother wants the Ashram to be. If
there is any disloyalty that must go. Some people question
too many things and this must be given up and we must
have faith and be faithful. Then she will lead us to the place
she wants us to go. The Mother's formula is "Be simple, be
happy."

*Do you believe that the Ashram and Auroville will
become more closely linked in time?*

You know Mother's presence is there always in the
Matrimandir. All outside matters will be sorted out in time.

There is much more closeness and harmony now than in past times. Each must know their role. Both are creations of the Mother and aspire ultimately for the same goal. What Mother starts cannot fail. The failure is in ourselves and our fixed opinions. This, and the ego, stand in the way and then it takes longer.

> *I was very close to your mother, Millie-di. She was such a pure soul. She had a light that was always shining from within. I used to love to sit with her in satsang and meditation at "Art House" during my visits. She passed on shortly after I left Pondicherry during my visit in 2001. Will you tell me what happened?*

She broke a bone just lying in bed in March 2001. She had an operation but her heart was very bad. The hip surgery went well, but an infection developed in a heart valve. She tried many medications but not a single medication worked. She tried everything. She was very cheerful in the nursing home. She painted and walked with her walker. On May 23, 2001, in the early morning, she passed away peacefully.

I used to tell her that she was a collector of children in the "Art House". In 1964 the Mother gave her blessings to start the "Art House". This had come out of her years of creating costumes for Ashram plays and the hand painting of Mother's saris. We all used to work there after school making beautiful hand painted saris, handkerchiefs and other designs. My mother was a great lover of beauty. She painted beautifully. My family members were painters, writers and musicians. Our family, when still living in Calcutta, used to put on productions with singing, dancing and drama. They would make a stage by joining beds and put on plays, dances and dramas. It was always a very lively place. At one point my Aunt Minnie went back to visit the old home and friends and all the neighbors said, "Since your family left the street has died, there is no more music. No more laughter."

As I entered the "Art House" I realized that it is only yourself, your Aunt Minnie and Chum remaining in this grand and stately house. As I sat waiting for you I could see all the lovely saris in the gift shop and all the works of art that continue to be created there and kept alive. I could still feel the presence of Millie-di. It was the same with Sunil as people still visit his music studio, buy his tapes and his beautiful music was heard wafting sweetly past my ears as I sat waiting for you on the verandah. It was a happy feeling. Will you speak about your uncle, Sunil Bhattacharya and his music?

He taught himself to play sitar. Although he studied science at St. Xavier's College in Bombay, he was an excellent football player, botanist and mathematician who taught in the Ashram school and he loved music. From 1945 he began composing musical pieces as accompaniments to dance performances. Eventually music became a means to his sadhana and he gave up teaching in the Ashram school after many years to devote himself full time to composing. From 1965 he was entrusted by the Mother to compose the New Year music, the theme of which she always gave him on his birthday on November 3rd. In 1966 Mother requested him to compose musical accompaniments for her *Savitri* readings, a work he continued until the end of his life. In the mid 1960s he recorded for Delhi Music Archives. He said, "The Mother revealed to me the secret world of music where harmonies meet and blend to make melodies richer, wider, profounder and infinitely more powerful. I have tried to take my music from her. My music is my labor and my aspiration for the Divine and what I try to convey through it are the voices of my inner experiences.

"My grateful thoughts are with her who has been my Guide, Guru, Mentor and Mother. One day it was her Light that sparked my heart, it is her Light that has sustained its glow, it is her Light that I seek through my music. If this music brings some comfort, some delight or some message to someone, I have achieved that for which she has placed her trust in me."

[Some comments made by the Mother on Sunil's music:

"Your music is, according to me, the music of the future and it opens the way to the New World." (13.8.65)

Again later she wrote:

"My child, yesterday at a quarter past twelve and again today, at the same time, I have heard your music with deep emotion and I can tell you that I have never heard anything more beautiful, in music, of aspiration and spiritual invocation."

Sunil passed away on April 30, 1999.]

> *Tell me about your years as a teacher in the Center of Education.*

When I was nine years old, the Mother told me she wanted me to be a teacher and at age eleven she said, "You will be a teacher." I started teaching French at age twenty to students age sixteen at the Centre of Education. I was teaching part time while I was still in school. The Mother said, "I am there to help you" and she did. She would suggest books on how to develop observation and understanding. Mother was continually giving me helpful guidelines. I could always write to her. Often when I would ask Mother a question she would say to me, "Do you want me to say yes, or do you want my opinion." I soon was teaching full-time. I taught French and English literature. Then I gradually moved on to teaching Sri Aurobindo's works, *Savitri*, *Life Divine* and Mother's *Entretiens*.

Tell me about what teaching is like for you in Knowledge, the higher course of the Ashram School.

As a teacher in Knowledge, we are somewhat at the mercy of the students. They are free to learn whatever they want and that is what we must teach. It is a form of the Free Progress system. If they want to read *Essays on the Gita* or *Synthesis*, then we, as teachers, must be adequately informed. Reading Sri Aurobindo's works at age thirty is different from reading him at age sixty. I have been teaching for forty years and it is never the same. There is always more to be learned. I am always changing my way of viewing things.

How have the students changed through the years?

The children are definitely changing. By the age of nine-teen, twenty, twenty-one, they have finished their higher courses. Thirty years ago age eighteen was simpler and yet somewhat more mature. Simpler in the sense that there was less outside influence and exposure. The world's values of today and its habits, customs, were not available to them then. Today's teens have access to outside influences. When I was young fifty years ago we were in a cocoon — more innocent. However, with Mother's presence there was a deeper development. The values of today's children are colored by what they see, read, feel. There is so much expo-sure to outside media and then they go home to Bombay and elsewhere for holidays. I am very grateful that my roots are based in the Ashram. Today most of the students leave the Ashram, whereas in past years they stayed on and be-came Ashramites. But mentally they are clearer. They know exactly what they want. Mostly they are taken up with ex-ternal things. The inner life has to be encouraged. They feel shy about inner things. They are so much more mental and of course technology has produced this. They all want to go out of the Ashram and obtain MBAs, go into business, com-puters, mass communications media and to make money. But Mother said that all the students are connected by a "Golden Chain" and even though they go out there is a tre-mendous bond between them and they always return for visits.

Can you offer a brief assessment of your sixty years of life in the Ashram and what it has meant for you?

I truly do not feel a sense of age. Also, I do not feel I have done anything myself except to open to the Mother and allow her to do everything for me as best I could. I just let her take charge at every step of the way with what had to be done for my sadhana. If there is something I have to transform i.e. ego problems, attachments and the like, I would visualize the image of Krishna and the Charioteer. I would just allow myself to be led and then my personal formula of "Remember and Offer" is always there. If the ego comes up one has to be persistent and say, "Let her decide, Let her decide."

Always circumstances come to reveal
the hidden weaknesses
that have to be overcome.

The Mother

Anurakta

Anurakta

(Manager of Sri Aurobindo Ashram Hand Made Paper and Occultist for the New Age)

In the mid-morning hours of Sunday December 22, 2002 I hailed a rickshaw and went bouncing along the dusty roads on the Bazaar side of the Pondicherry canal heading towards Sri Aurobindo Ashram Hand Made Paper. The paper factory is north of the main Ashram compound and is situated in the midst of a dense and cool grove of coconut palms forever thick with a battalion of pesky little mosquitoes buzzing around and ready for attack.

Anurakta, whose name was given by the Mother, and means Lovingly Devoted — One Enamoured, is a sensitive man with a round face and fair skin. His eyes are deep blue and though he speaks with a slight stammer he has great inner strength and possesses a highly developed capacity for mental concentration.

We have been friends for many years and when I arrived he was quietly sitting in his small cottage nestled in the grounds of the paper factory. We had known one another since the early 1960s when Narad, Eleanor Montgomery, Sam Spanier and I formed a business in New York for importing the Ashram's hand made paper. We sat and reminisced about the paper business days also remembering our mutual friend, the late Marilyn Widman, from New York City, who had lived in the Ashram for many years and worked for Sri A.B. Patel in the World Union publication offices. The three of us used to sit in the Government Park and talk about sadhana and people as we watched the myriad forms of life move past us engaged in their repeated daily round of activities. There were small, thin Tamil men in bullock carts, beggars, pigs, goats, hungry, wild-looking dogs with exposed rib bones, motor-bikes, mopeds, rickshaws, bicycles, naked babies and dark skinned women and children in brightly colored clothing. Pondicherry was then and still is, an ongoing festival of sights and sounds and smells.

I conducted the interview in Anurakta's Puja room where all his statues of the Hindu pantheon of Gods and Goddesses sit immobile in their power poses. He dresses them ornately in jewels and rich, silk saris. They stared piercingly into the atmosphere as though they were privy to my innermost thoughts. The room was permeated with their electrical energy, yet there existed, also, a palpable calm. After a moment of quiet reflection I put the following questions to Anurakta:

Where were you born?

I was born Anthony David Rochelle in Bournemouth, England on February 5, 1932.

What is the history and background of your family? What were their religious beliefs?

My mother's side of the family was rural and they were farmers from the west of England. My father's people were brewers from the north of England whose ancestors had originally come from France to escape religious persecutions. I did not know my paternal grandfather. My mother's father was a watch and clock repairman. My religion was Congregational Methodist. It was no more than a formality and tradition. After my grandfather died I went to church mostly alone.

What were your special talents? What were your childhood ambitions?

I had no special talents. My parents split up at the beginning of world war II and after many difficulties my mother re-married in order to give my sister and me a home. I did not like her husband and having developed a stammer I began writing poetry. I knew nothing about other religions but wanted early on to be a hermit in Arabia or a "tramp" (vagabond or gypsy) in England! At one time I entertained the idea of entering the church ministry but the stammer ended that. I also wanted to be a fashion designer.

Were you aware of a spiritual presence in your childhood and when did you first aspire deeply for the spiritual life?

I was slightly aware as I had one or two uplifting experiences in church as a child but I began to aspire for a truly spiritual life in East Africa in my late twenties when I discovered Hinduism.

How do you see your early life as being influential to

your coming to the Yoga of Sri Aurobindo?

Non-attachment! I also now realize the Divine hand that was
involved in taking a stammering nineteen-year-old to Central Africa who then hitch-hiked through Central East Africa to Kenya and later on to an exploration of India in 1960.

*How did you learn of Mother and Sri Aurobindo and
when did you come to live in the Ashram?*

I was told about Mother and Sri Aurobindo in Nairobi,
Kenya. I attended some meetings there and planned a
month's visit to the Ashram in 1960.

*Can you describe darshan of the Mother? What
experiences did you have with her?*

Darshan of the Mother always overwhelmed me. She appeared to be so vast and all-powerful. But I never truly felt a
personal intimacy with her.

Why not? What does that mean exactly?

Well, when I heard about people putting their heads on her
lap or writing to her and closing with "Your child", I found
this difficult. I saw her as the Universal Mother rather than
the personal Mother. I had more of a psychic relationship
with both Mother and Sri Aurobindo. They were both very
much in my heart center.

   In 1960, when I visited, I had asked her if I could stay on.

She did not grant this wish at that time. However, in July 1961, through Ambu, she called me to come.

Straightaway from the day of my arrival, she gave me my work in the paper factory. The next week I went to her salon darshan. I saw that everybody had a rose to give her and I had nothing so I felt inspired to take off my grandfather's gold wedding ring, which I wore, and gave it to her instead of a rose. She looked most surprised!

Later my colleague, Reba, and I went to have her darshan on the last day of every month in her top floor room. I was trying to develop our stationery section and each month I would take Mother a new design of stationery. She always displayed the greatest delight and pleasure over it. At that time we had a very good gardener at the paper factory and on my birthdays he would always prepare a huge bouquet of flowers, leaves and ferns for me to take with me for Mother. One year I decided the customary single red rose would be more appropriate as my huge bouquet seemed to drop leaves all over me and appeared so untidy. But a friend who worked with Mother reported that when my name was read out from the birthday list for the coming week she said, "He always brings me such a lovely bouquet." So it continued in this way.

One year when my birthday was on a Monday I went with a friend on the Sunday before and gathered white lotus flowers from a village pond. I looked after them as best I could. When I finally got into her room for her blessings the lotuses looked to me to be very bedraggled and pathetic. But Mother received them with enormous pleasure, which of course lifted me up and up.

When I first had a balcony darshan of the Mother it seems that she said to Sri Madhav Pandit, "Does that man know about occultism?" Madhav said, "I don't think so." Mother said, "Behind him there stands a tall, dark figure." Was it Kali?

In the late 1960s I had begun to work with self-hypnosis. I experimented with past life regression and as far back as I could remember. Suddenly I saw that I had been a herdsman in Central Asia (Afghanistan or Mongolia) north of the Himalayas. I had been grazing cattle for the summer and had come back to my village. I had been experimenting with black magic and upon return to my village my young wife intuited changes in me and knew of the black magic practices. She would have nothing to do with me and I was an outcast in the community. I then went higher into the foothills and lived as a sadhu, as a hermit growing my own food, and found an ancient goddess figure statue. An arm fell from the statue onto my body and killed me. In my subsequent life my being was searching for the "goddess". When I found Mother I realized her to be the goddess figure I was worshipping and to whom I wished to be totally surrendered. Later on the Mother confirmed this. After this surrender Mother and Sri Aurobindo put another being into my body for my spiritual growth and I became more Hindu-oriented. This was all realized towards the end of the 1960s.

Could you describe the atmosphere of the Ashram when Mother was still in her physical body and the difference since that time?

I feel the main differences are 1) daily life from the balcony darshan onwards focussed on and around Mother's physical presence. We also had to ask permission for everything i.e. to go to Madras, etc. Everything for our sadhana and work was decided by the Mother. 2) Now the Ashram is larger, the work is perhaps more demanding and complex and there are many more visitors. The samadhi was always peaceful and with relatively few people praying and meditating there. Now it is always crowded. Pondicherry itself is much noisier and larger which affects our daily life. We are therefore drawn inwards much more with a deeper compulsion to realize Mother and Sri Aurobindo on an inner level within ourselves. If one is sincere one is compelled to find her inside. When she was here there was much more concern with her outwardly. It was said that when Mother left her body it was easier for those ashramites to adjust who had little daily contact with her physically, and who had already strongly established the inner contact, as opposed to those who dealt with her on a daily basis for business and the like.

What has life been like for you since Mother left her body? In what way has your sadhana changed?

My inner life, devotion and aspiration are now more concentrated. Naturally, with age, one develops more deeply the spiritual sense.

What changes do you see taking place in the Ashram in the future? In the same manner what do you see in Auroville's future? Will the two creations of the Mother work more closely together?

For the Ashram outwardly, perhaps, there will be no great
changes from now on but certainly a deeper yogic intensity
and integral progress will manifest in more and more disciples. Mother's living presence and continual guidance is always there — strong and positive.

For Auroville at some time in the future I see a vaster
occult splendor and a deeper inner sense of union with the
Ashram.

What do you see specifically?

It will become necessary for some people to do a deeper
tapasya. The raw physical-vital forces present in the very
land of Auroville must be dealt with. This has not been dealt
with sufficiently. The Matrimandir will have a tremendous
effect on this. Auroville land is of the raw earth. In the surrounding villages the deities are simple, rural and primitive.
The concerns are for crops, food, rainfall and so forth. The
spirits are very elemental. These reigning deities resent a
push towards transformation and change. These old occult
powers see people moving away from ancient practices, devotion to old deities and going towards the future and the
new creation. Some intense tapasya is needed by residents
of Auroville in order to correct this and to help Auroville
become more grounded in the Presence of Mother and Sri
Aurobindo.

Occultism has not been a part of Ashram life. Mother felt
it would be misused. One must have little or no ego to prac-

tice occultism. Ancient occultism has become dark. Occultism for the New Age needs new light, force and a higher vibration.

Has your guidance from Mother and Sri Aurobindo revealed anything to you about the Western world and its spiritual progress?

The Western world is burdened by its subconscious memories and its past. It is all sadly complex.

What do you mean by this? What are those subconscious memories?

For instance there is great agony in the German people as they sit on the subconscious memories of their terrible history of warfare and conflict. Other Europeans feel similarly with regard to their histories.

America is truly an escape route to freer understanding of life. It is a place of refuge. It has a good future and a very important role to play. America has more physical space than Europe and this is useful and helpful to the human spirit. An expansion of physical space is more helpful for the inner life.

Also the Western world is burdened by an over-emphasis on mental constructions. It seems that Science drags its mental feet with no sense, yet, of exploration of the higher regions of the mind as outlined by Sri Aurobindo. Also the Western world seems to need a stronger sense of Bhakti [devotion], a deeper spiritual adoration of the Divine. This will come about through Indian leadership.

   How?

Through a process of contact with the Eastern thought
by reading Sri Aurobindo. In Russia now Satprem's *Sri
Aurobindo* or *the Adventure of Consciousness* has had tremendous outreach and George Van Vrekhem's *Beyond the
Human Species* is also widely read in the West. The teachings of Sri Ramakrishna and Sri Aurobindo and other influences from the East have been enormously beneficial for
the West. They are breaking down the great divisions and
narrowness that existed between the two cultures.

   *Would you give advice to new spiritual aspirants that
   would help in their development and help them to
   integrate their lives in the world with its focus on
   materialism and the vital life, or is each better off
   seeking their own way?*

My main advice is:
   1) Silence the mind by concentrating on Sri Aurobindo's
name and allow the breathing to become slower and deeper.
   2) Imagine, discover and realize the presence of the
Mother in the heart center. When one can surrender to her in
the heart, she takes up the Yoga of Transformation from that
level in the way she knows to be the best.
   3) Try to surrender one's past — all of it, as the Mother
surrendered to Sri Aurobindo. This also helps in purifying
the subconscious.

4) Read from the beginning. Don't begin, as many do, with the *Agenda*. When I asked Mother in 1961 what I should read first, she said *Essays on the Gita*.

Is there a disadvantage in never having seen Mother in her physical body?

Surely there must be. She could look at you deeply and know who you were and choose the right work for you. I would not have chosen the paper factory for myself. I would have said "Put me in the library", or something like that. But to have been given your special work by the Mother was very important and helpful. In around 1971 I wrote to the Mother asking her about my work in the Paper Department. She said " It is a time of good work and sincerity. Continue." I have gained so much by simply doing that and not listening to other people's advice and guidance. The Handmade Paper Department has developed enormously. In the beginning I did the posting, banking, typing, attendance record, accounting, designing and all. Now we have a huge export market and staff, but it is she who is behind it all. This is always absolutely very obvious and clear to me.

How did you come to be directed to practice occultism and healing?

In December of 1979 I went to a book fair and found a book on the I CHING. I was most interested in how, by dividing up the sticks, one could get answers. Was it coming from the subconscious or was it the higher consciousness? I asked this question. Also in 1979, after many years, I visited England again. Returning to India I purchased a book in the airport on occultism in England. There was a section on divining (water divining). In Ambu's room I took cotton and hung it over an apple and with a ring I made a pendulum. To my astonishment it moved largely. This had a strong impact on me. I went into this study more deeply. When I developed this I did not settle with "Yes" and "No" and "I don't know" answers. I hung the pendulum over objects and wrote words and watched its movements. I analyzed this and discovered there were twelve specific movements of the pendulum that mean inner harmony, outer harmony, outer actions, inner actions, etc. You have to get the exact meaning and you have to count the number of times it gives the same action. If there are fifteen movements up and down it is a "hill" and if there are fifty movements it is "the Himalayas"!! I kept a notebook of all these analyses. With the help of the pendulum I could look at handwriting and photographs and know what kind of person it was. If someone wanted to see me and there was a very negative force, sometimes I would have to reject seeing them and discourage a meeting, but not often. I felt I had a duty to the Mother to see and help everyone who came to me.

Mother approved this work fairly early on and guided me in it. One could be connecting with the pendulum to lower powers, but early on I started my sessions with mantras given by the Mother. I always refer to Mother and Sri Aurobindo in this work. It is necessary to be careful to maintain a silent mind. Any mental agitation must be stopped. If there is a mental formation it can influence the movement of the pendulum. I began by using the circle of ABC's from the middle of the circle. I silence the mind, then I can hear Mother softly speaking. I use the pendulum for signature readings and to check for right answers. I only do this in my office or room, not in people's homes. The pendulum is the key for me to the silencing of the mind and then to the receptivity to the Mother's guidance. More and more she helps and guides people from many parts of India — mostly family problems. I place a lot of importance on Sri Aurobindo's name as a mantra.

This basic knowledge and ability led me to the consciousness of stones — especially granite, as a result of which I have acquired statues and small stones for "research". Also I work with the healing power of numbers in the form of mantras and yantras.

If I pick up a stone, I put the pendulum over the stone. If it is an ordinary stone it gives off ten to fifteen movements. I put the pendulum over the stone, then I keep the stone touching the photo of Mother for several hours after which the pendulum begins to register up to three hundred movements. At the Ramana Maharshi Ashram in the Arunachala mountains, sacred to Lord Shiva, every stone picked up there is blazing with light and energy. The Samadhi also radiates these kinds of power waves to transform the earth.

An Ashram woman has been helping me with this research. We kept stones in different colored boxes, each stone vibrated differently. We came to realize that the surface of the stone changes but its core remains the same.

Someone came to a shop with a sapphire and wanted to sell it. The sapphire belonged to a family who had nothing

left and needed the money. It had been in the forehead of a
goddess in a temple and some ancestor had stolen it. It wasn't
sold because people in India don't wear sapphires. It ended
up in Pondicherry and they put it in a bank vault. The elder
daughter, who was friendly with me, said there was something wrong in their lives, no one was getting married. She
told me the story of the sapphire. She showed it to me and I
measured it — it was positively evil, with a terrible vibration! I asked her to leave it with me overnight to be placed by
Mother's photo. The next day it was normal. The Mother had
absorbed the violence from it. I advised the girl not to keep it
but to place it in the Smithsonian Museum. This was not done.
They kept the stone and it absorbed the bad vibration again.
The family continues to experience bad luck to this day.

There are thousands of souls in need of help; health, marriage, education, finances. In Orissa there are more people
concerned with their inner lives. By and large it is mostly
Indians who come to me.

How do you protect yourself?

I receive an average of five letters per day, as well as phone
calls and e-mails seeking guidance and personal consulta-
tions. This can be very tiring.

I use the Mother's mantra. I surrender to her. She answers
the letters. Two hours is the absolute maximum I can work.
While working this way I am okay. If I need to make any
changes I seek help from the Mother.

I will tell you a story:

A man came from Orissa; a tall, handsome man who had
an Ashram there.

He had linked up with a tantric guru in New Delhi who had disciples in New Delhi. This guru gave him a tantric mantra and the man went home and for two to three months for eight hours a day he repeated the mantra! After some time he began shouting and screaming and had completely lost control. He kept ranting and screaming. He checked with his guru in New Delhi and found that one syllable in the mantra was mispronounced. From this mistake had come a violent reaction in him.

Afterwards he went to Ramakrishna Mission and ultimately to Mother and Sri Aurobindo. When he next came to see me he said, "What is the best thing for me?" I told him to repeat Sri Aurobindo's name and then all would be okay. This is the sort of work that I do.

I am also working more with numbers now for access to occult powers. The Mother had told me, "Don't do what has been done before." There are new ways of becoming more aware of the occult worlds. The protection is needed when one is doing the Integral Yoga in particular. Extra power, force and protection are needed and numbers are one way of achieving this. I am not a visionary person. One cannot have all the powers to be had, but my vital being can detach itself and travel off to other levels. Some years ago I flew over the Himalayas. I went to a spot in Central Asia. When I entered a doorway there was a long hall full of men from around the world; bankers, politicians. In an alcove was the leader whom I initially did not see. I came through the door and sat down. They spoke of attacking and destroying the world, commerce, etc. One man started to verbally attack Sri Aurobindo. I stood up and retaliated. Everyone looked and said, "Who is he?"

Then the being in the alcove said, "Catch him." I flew out of the door, chased by all these people. I flew over China and crossed the Himalayas and they could not follow. India has a special protection and they fell back, exhausted. Is this something to be feared? This evil can be conquered with enough spiritual knowledge. We may condemn Western commerce and industry for expanding globally, but it will have a very beneficial effect. There is at present so much darkness in the world.

> *Now that you are in your seventies, what has yoga done for you at this stage in your life? Can you give me an assessment of your forty-plus years in the Ashram?*

I feel that I have grown tremendously within. I often use the pendulum on my own signature. When I came here I was just a simple but sincere young seeker. Now I have more ability, knowledge and have learned how to develop a silent mind. I repeat Mother and Sri Aurobindo's names as a mantra and feel their presence always.

Mother said, "Never stop striving for perfection." This is a strong motto for my life and one that motivates my life and work and sadhana.

Anurakta with Dieties in his puja room, Aug. 1995

Kali deity and other statues, Aug. 1995

W 13

Anu Purani

Anu Purani

*(Dancer, Choreographer, Writer and Teacher in
Auroshikha's Udavi Village School)*

Anu Purani is the only daughter of the late A.B. Purani, one
of Sri Aurobindo's original disciples, who was the recorder
of *Evening Talks with Sri Aurobindo*, and author of *Sri
Aurobindo's Integral Yoga, The Life of Sri Aurobindo* and
other publications. He was also a Sanskrit scholar.

Anu is small with a petite frame and a dancer's lithe and
supple body. She also moves with the grace and agility of a
dancer; her back is straight, her head is held high and she has
a turn of her feet reminiscent of ballet dancers in fifth position. She lives in the main Ashram compound near the
Samadhi above what used to be the fruit room.

She was born in Surat, Gujarat, on January 5th. She told
me that the year is unknown as her parents kept shifting her
horoscope, but it is supposed to have been around the mid
1920s. She was brought to the Ashram when she was an infant at which time she and her mother joined her father who
was already in residence there.

Anu told me that she had been very close to her father and
that to her he was like a demi-god. She said that he was a
very good father, teacher and a great human being. As a result of this closeness she spoke quite openly to me about him
and in this interview her remembrances are lovingly detailed.

She told me that prior to his coming to the Ashram, while

he was still in high school in Gujarat, he saw Sri Aurobindo in Baroda and when Sri Aurobindo gave a lecture he went to hear him. After seeing Sri Aurobindo he later told his friends that he felt Sri Krishna had again taken birth. At that time he was convinced that it was his destiny to follow him. Sri Aurobindo was planning a revolution in India. The British Raj was still in power and at that time, around the turn of the century, nearly all of India was colonized by the British. Sri Aurobindo was looking for strong young men who could prepare the district of Gujarat for the revolution to free India from the British. Anu said Sri Aurobindo selected her father and her uncle (his brother) and they were both quite willing to work in this capacity. While Purani was in college he started physical culture centers all over Gujarat for sports, body-work, playing sticks, climbing wooden poles and wrestling. At that time there were many young men from Afghanistan who knew wrestling well and her father approached them and asked them to teach him wrestling. They would not do this so he decided to make a hole in the wall of their studio while they were practising and learn from them in this manner! Eventually he brought this sport and art form to his centers and taught it himself. After college he said he would not take a job so long as India was not free. He slept on the sidewalks during this period. His centers did not generate income at that time, but soon his work attracted the Indian Home Minister and other popular politicians of the day began to notice him. They were expecting him to be helpful with the Freedom Movement.

All this while he was communicating with Sri Aurobindo and he finally came to Pondicherry to meet him in 1923. He told Sri Aurobindo, "Now we are ready. What is the next step?" Sri Aurobindo said, "Drop it." Purani said, "What shall I do?" Sri Aurobindo replied, "Start practising yoga."

Sri Aurobindo told him, "My experience with this movement has made it clear that India's freedom will be brought about by some other means." Purani asked, "But will India be free?" Sri Aurobindo replied, "Yes, it will be free." Purani was not certain and he asked him again, "What guarantee can you give me?" Sri Aurobindo stood up and looked far off into the distance and said, "India's freedom is as certain as the rising of the sun tomorrow." Purani responded, "Now after many years I shall sleep well tonight."

A.B. Purani then came to live in the Ashram, but he caused a scandal in Gujarat. All the people who had supported him and followed him for the work of the Freedom Movement felt betrayed and letters of complaint were written to him in the Ashram. However, the Divine had other plans for him.

Tell me about your early days in the Ashram.

Well, I was just an infant and there was actually not much of an Ashram community at that time and no school. I remember one story that my father told about me when I was still in the crawling stage. My father's quarters were just across from Sri Aurobindo's rooms. The talks with sadhaks would take place in the evenings. The sadhaks meditated, also, with Sri Aurobindo and perhaps I heard them speaking about meditation. Sometimes, as Sri Aurobindo's room had swinging doors, I would crawl into Sri Aurobindo's room and settle into a chair. My father would come looking for me and apologize to Sri Aurobindo and ask me, "What are you doing?" I would say "jeu jeu". At times doors to both quarters were left open. One night I crawled from my father's flat into Sri Aurobindo's rooms and I was heard repeating the words "dana", "dana". It was surmised that I had heard the sadhaks during these evening talks discussing sadhana so often that I was trying to imitate the sound of the word!

When I was about a year old I fell ill and was sent to the hospital in Madras. It was during the intense summer heat. I had a high fever, boils and my entire body was swollen. The Mother said, "The atmosphere is too intense, this child cannot live here." I was sent back to Gujarat to live with my grandparents. It was not easy to send a year-old child away but this was an indication of my parents' faithfulness to the guru. I stayed with my grandparents until I was seven years old. They were middle class people and had a temple in their home. There were no children around. There was an elder aunt who looked after me. She was a mother to me. All that while I did not see my parents, not once.

My first playmates were little statues of gods and goddesses. I gave them flowers and talked to them and prepared sandal paste for them. It was a very lovely childhood. When I was about age seven my mother came back to my grandparents. She was a new person to me. I did not really know her and furthermore I did not especially like her. Her name was Lila. One day I said, "Why don't you go back to your home? Why are you staying here?" Then my Auntie said, "But, she is your mother." My aunt brought me closer to my

Anu as a child in the Ashram

Anu in front of her Ashram Quarters, Dec. 2002

mother but it took a long time. She said, "You loved only your father and always only wanted to play with him." I lived with my mother from seven to ten years of age and then we returned to the Ashram when I was age ten.

I loved my father very much and remember once saying to him (probably in a moment of needing his attention), "You know, I am your only child, your only daughter!" He kept quiet for a few minutes, then he said, "Don't boast. You are not the only daughter I have. I have many daughters all over the world." I thought now he is boasting! But when he fell ill so many people wrote him letters asking if there was anything they could do for him. People sent money and their good wishes. People would write to him from all over asking for advice and help. He tried to answer all of them himself. Lois Duncan [an American disciple from Sedona, Arizona] worshipped him. She and her husband, Nicholas, brought him to America in 1964 for a series of lectures throughout the United States. My father passed away in the Ashram in 1965 one year after his visit to America.

He left me with a great gift — a deep love for India. I pray every day for India to come into her own true power after so many years of British rule.

What were your school days like in the Ashram?

When the Mother used to meet with the children of the Ashram in the playground, once she asked us, "What do you think God is?" She told us nothing could really perfectly describe what God is. She said, "One could say perfection, or light, or beauty and yet it really wouldn't completely describe what God is." In a series of meetings she spoke about evolution and she told us children about the beginnings of life in the ocean and how some life forms began to evolve into amphibians and then set forth onto the land. Someone asked her about the birds. She said, "That was a special expression, not from the earth, not from the sea but from another plane of existence." Someone asked about the evolution of man from the monkey. She said the evolution of man was the result of a direct intervention from the Divine. She also said that the fact that all other animals looked down but that Homo sapiens stood erect and looked up is symbolic of the capacity to look at things from above.

For the classes in the school she was not keen on the students learning Sri Aurobindo's philosophy. Much later it was Tanmaya [a French-Swiss teacher in the Ashram school for many years] who wanted to educate the children in a different way. Instead of having classes following the teacher, the teachers would follow the students. This was the beginning of the Free Progress system. If a child asked a question and it led to some other subject it was okay. The Mother said if a child did not want to study he or she was free to be ignorant. It did not mean that they had no other faculties or capacities. So some learned electricity and became engineers. Some went into physical culture and other areas of study. Not everybody liked the Free Progress method. At present Sri Aurobindo is taught in the Higher Course at "Knowledge" and Free Progress is a choice, it is not imposed. The systems are parallel, not everyone has the kind of mentality to take up Free Progress. One needs to have a willing and

keen mind to acquire knowledge. One must be willing to
work hard.

When did you take up dance study formally?

After finishing my education in the Ashram school I began
formal dance study. My father saw that I was restless and
fidgety. One day he said, "Uday Shankar [brother of the
famed Sitarist, Ravi Shankar] is dancing in Madras." He sent
me to see the company perform. I was just sixteen years old
and it was the first time I had ever experienced a profes-
sional dance company. It was so thrilling that I could not
sleep that night. I wanted to go away and study dance and
there was a big tussle between father and daughter. My father said he could not let me leave the Ashram. I said, "I
don't care, I am going." This went on between us and he
also told me he had no money. How could he help me? Finally the Mother said, "Purani, let her go." With some help
from wealthy friends of his in Gujarat he finally sent me to
Kalakshetra School of Dance in Madras. He said, "I cannot
let you go far away." The lady managing the school was
Rukmini Devi. She was closely connected with the Theo-
sophical Society in Madras. I stayed in a hostel with other
dancers. It was a big dormitory room. There I learned
Bharatanatyam dance [the classical dance of India] and was
well liked by Rukmini Devi. I was there for two years and
came back to the Ashram for holidays. Then I received a
pamphlet from Uday Shankar in Almora, in the foothills of
the Himalayan mountains. It was a beautiful, hilly paradise.
He had a dance school there for the summer months. I joined

Sri A.B. Purani (Anu's father) with Tulsi offering for
Sri Aurobindo

up. After I arrived and started the program, he told us that
Bharata Natyam had no real meaning. He told us we must
find our own way of dancing. The first thing he did was to
make us walk. Then he would say, "Why are you looking
down?" He wanted us all to walk around with our heads up
and look at him. Then he would count and count and count
and then demonstrate. He would say, "Think and then do."
Then he would say, "When I say start dancing you start."
He wanted immediate rhythmic precision. He wanted us to
start in the exact moment of the count. We used to dance for
eight hours straight, then exercise one hour, then rest one
hour in the afternoon. At night we would start at 7 p.m. He
would take the entire school in a circle and play music for
us. He would ask us what the music meant. He would ask us

Sri A.B. Purani in New York 1964 with Eric Hughes, Anie,
Kailas, Matilda Scott, Sam Spanier, Dr. Karelitz-Karry,
Mrs. Polly Holmes, Mrs. Eleanor Montgomery

what it was telling us. He wanted us to feel the emotion of
the music for ourselves, to experience it on our own. I stayed
with him for two years. He took us on tours all over India.
We danced in so many places, then World War II broke out.
As a result of the war the money he was receiving to help
the company stay alive ceased.

Shankar wanted to act in a film about his life that he was
to direct. He wanted us all to be in it, but we did not agree
with it. There was a big fight between Shankar and the dance
troupe because we refused. We had an engagement in the
capitol of Gujarat. Everything was already booked. We were
all young and hard-headed and we did him a great injustice
for we all cancelled out and left him in the lurch one day in
advance of the performance date. He had to organize some

other program for the audiences. Of course he wrote an angry letter to my father, but I had just gone along with the group decision. After this experience I returned to the Ashram. I was twenty years old.

What did you do after you returned to Pondicherry?

The Mother had asked me to join the embroidery group with Mona, Pushpa, Kusum and others. We embroidered bedspreads and other linen for Golconde Guest House. After six months there she asked me to iron some clothes in the school dormitory for twenty children who were boarding there. She then told me that I could be in charge of the dormitory and look after the children. I had never thought of marriage and family life, but like my father I loved children. I was very happy working there. Kusum and I worked together, then she became ill and had to go home. I was left all alone with this work. One day I was going upstairs and the Mother opened her door. I was thinking how lucky I was to have so many children. At that moment Mother said, "How good it is that you have so many children." I wondered how she could know exactly what I was thinking.

Then she asked me to start dance classes. I did both these things simultaneously. She selected the music for me. I composed my own type of dances and she was so generous with her praise. That continued for twenty years. Then in 1976-77 Maggi Lidchi-Grassi [one of Mother's secretaries and the author of many books] approached me about teaching in the newly formed Udavi village school outside Pondicherry. The Udavi school was established by Maggi Lidchi-Grassi and her late husband, Nata Grassi, who had also founded Auroshikha incense factory. Udavi, in Tamil language, means "Help" and the name was given by the Mother. The Auroshikha factory was, at that time, on the grounds of the school but has since moved to Pondicherry.

By 1978 I was fully involved as a teacher at Udavi. In 1983-84 Maggi went to America for a long stay and I was asked to take over as chief superintendent of the school. I had full reign at that time. I had a very loving relationship with Maggi and the students. A new plot of land was purchased and another building put up. We had a wall built around the buildings so that goats and cows could not come in.

I have greatly expanded inwardly from my experience at Udavi. As a child I received loving affection from family but something was lacking. I tried to be friendly but had no discrimination. My father used to say, "Don't be like the mythical bird that looks at every passing cloud and follows it, one who can only drink rain water and no other water. Be more practical and not so idealistic." So there at Udavi, with the children, I had my first experience of unselfish, impersonal love. I felt they were all my children. I was so proud of them. I knew some would go to college and one boy even entered the army. It was total, unconditional love on my part towards them.

Sanjeev Agarwal of SAIIER (Sri Aurobindo International Institute of Educational Research) in Auroville came to see what the children were doing. He saw them acting, dancing, reciting and he was impressed. Soon the school was placed under the management of SAIIER (though the Ashram is still financially responsible) and Sanjeev asked me to be the director of the school.

What can you say about Auroville, its growth and development, its future and relationship with the Ashram?

When Auroville was being built there was great enthusiasm in the Ashram and many people went out to help. Then, due to some problems and ensuing court cases and for other unknown reasons, something happened. The Aurovilians suddenly did not want ashramites going there anymore. This was in the early 1980s. I was teaching dance at the Last School in Auroville. The ashramites became blocked from being in Auroville and I also stopped my classes. I do not know if it was some idea of competition, a political matter of positions or what the cause was, but things escalated and there are still some problems existing today. Some Aurovilians have not learned to use absolute freedom in the highest way. Hopefully the existence of the Savitri Bhavan and Matrimandir will change that situation, then Auroville will come around to more yogic ways.

How has your sadhana changed since Mother and Sri Aurobindo are no longer in their physical bodies?

Now I must rely on myself. I have to go more deeply within myself to find the answers and solutions to situations.

Would you describe your darshans with Mother and

> *Sri Aurobindo and any remembrances that you have of*
> *the Mother?*

Once Mother asked me to dance and in the story I had to
conquer the asura [evil power]. The asura was attracted to
me and he wanted to conquer me. I found this to be so difficult. Nothing seemed right in the way of dance movements.
Usually I hear a sound within my head indicating the correct choreographic movement. It is like a bell inside me.
But that bell never rang. I went to the Mother and I started
to cry. She then showed me the correct movements herself.
So, I repeated them in front of her and she said, "Yes, that is
it!" She would come to see the dress rehearsals and she saw
me on the stage. She asked me to dance again and I thought
that was the greatest compliment anyone could receive so I
happily danced for her again.

Upon returning to the Ashram from the Himalayas I
had many significant meetings with the Mother. It is very
difficult to describe them. I remember trembling all over
when I saw Mother and Sri Aurobindo on darshan days. Once
the Mother asked me, after one of the darshans (Sri
Aurobindo was still here at that time), "How was the darshan?
For what do you ask?" I said, "Mother, I do not ask anything." She said, "Every step you take you may always ask
for something." So, one day I asked her if Sri Aurobindo was
pleased with me. She said, "Yes." I asked, "Why doesn't he
smile at me?" Mother said, "He doesn't smile, but he is
pleased." This would be the last darshan that I would have of
Mother and Sri Aurobindo together.

I could see that Sri Aurobindo was uneasy and uncomfortable. I felt like going quickly. Then he looked straight at me and smiled. His look completely stopped me and I began to cry and cry. Something told me that I would not see him again. This was November 24, 1950 and of course he withdrew from his body on December 5, 1950.

> *What has life here in the Ashram meant to you? How has your life in this surcharged atmosphere and in the presence of Mother and Sri Aurobindo changed you?*

I can only say that I was a rather selfish person with a somewhat small personality.

The Mother has made me unselfish and removed certain limitations and widened my vision. She has helped me to feel one with India, one with the people with whom I work and to feel a great sense of love. I am no longer the person that I once was.

I still have many dreams and creative visions. One dream is to choreograph the dance-drama "Jonathan Livingston Seagull". I want to find a boy dancer who can leap all the way across the stage like a great bird. I am looking for this dancer.

Sanskritists use very few words to express large ideas. They say "Charaiveti, charaiveti", which means "Keep on moving, keep on moving!"

Aster Patel

Aster Patel

Aster Patel is a beautiful, sophisticated woman who can always be seen dressed in the most immaculately exquisite saris. One cannot help but notice just how perfectly coiffed is her trademark silvery hair. Her speech is soft and gentle, her movements feminine and graceful, but inwardly she is a warrior soul in her pursuit of the practice of the Integral Yoga. The redolent aura of her beauty carries with it a sense of the beauty and presence of the Mother. Aster had told us that as a young girl in the Ashram, she watched the Mother with fascination — how she carried herself, how she moved and how she displayed beauty in all she touched.

And she was irresistibly drawn to the splendor of that beauty.

Aster was born in New Delhi on March 17, 1932 and was given the name Mira by her renowned father, the eminent Indian psychologist and philosopher, Dr. Indra Sen. Later on her name was changed to Aster by the Mother. It is remarkable to note here that Dr. Sen named his daughter Mira (the same name as the Mother) before ever having met the Mother or knowing anything about her. After years of seeking the company of spiritual personalities and searching for the right Master, Dr. Sen was led to Sri Aurobindo, along with his good friend, Surendra Nath Jauhar. He turned to Sri Aurobindo in 1938 and in 1945 left his post as professor of Philosophy and Psychology at the University of Delhi to come and live permanently in the Ashram. His wife and two children had gone there two years prior in 1943.

My interview with Aster, unlike all the others which were conducted in India, took place in my home in Los Angeles following the annual national conference of all the devotees of Sri Aurobindo and the Mother in America called the AUM Conference (All USA Meeting). The East-West Cultural Center — The Sri Aurobindo Center of Los Angeles had been the host for the AUM 2003 that took place at Loyola Marymount University from May 22-26th. Aster was one of the guest speakers from India and stayed with me for three days afterward so that I could interview her. However, her understanding was that I was to question her about her knowledge of Ashram elders, not that she was to be a subject of the interview book herself! Being the quiet, private, unassuming person that she is *she froze*! She literally could not speak. Without knowing this, but sensing something, my friend Stuart inexplicably and suddenly appeared in the room and began telling Aster of the importance and need to relate her personal experiences and how vital it was to share her life's experiences of the Ashram, with the Mother and Sri Aurobindo and in Auroville and how it would be a source of inspiration for other seekers of the Integral Yoga for many years to come. This helped her to open up and over a two day period I transcribed eight hours of a flow of words that spun out like threads of pure silk until at the end of the eight hours it ceased, suddenly, in the same miraculous manner in which it had been initiated. It was an intense experience for both of us. Herewith is her experience, in her own words:

The atmosphere of my early childhood in New Delhi was

that of an intense concentration which marked my father's being. We were surrounded by many books and by other men of learning and his favourite students who never left him. He was professor of Psychology and Philosophy at the University of Delhi and a man of total dedication. Even as a child one could feel that he was on a deep quest. My mother carried the atmosphere of utter femininity. She was an Indian woman in the truest sense. She had a sweetness and a loving and caring way and, at the same time, was unobtrusive in her firmness and clarity — and with a strong basis of a sort of "substance" and "focus" that, at that age, I could not understand. She was also highly educated. She was the first woman graduate of Delhi University and won a gold medal in general studies. She was good at math and child psychology and became the principal of a large girls' school in New Delhi. She was a writer of short stories in Hindi and took part in radio programs and was interested in fine arts — dance, music, classical films, etc. She also had a great love for Bengali literature. The larger setting of our family was one of great reverence for spiritual personalities in general, who were always guests at our house. I was very conscious of this atmosphere. From an early age I had the feeling that I did not belong to the world as it was. The social aspect of household life did not appeal to me. It had no reality for me.

When did your family arrive in the Ashram?

My father had the fullness of satisfaction on an intellectual level with regard to his work. But he said, "I don't want to spend my whole life *talking* about God, I want to *know* Him." He wanted a spiritual realization — in experience — of the truths that psychology and philosophy try to reach conceptually. He travelled to different parts of the country in search of the Master who could lead him to that goal. In December of 1938, in the company of his close friend, Surendra Nath Jauhar, my father went to Pondicherry. That trip marked the end of his quest. The next year he went with my mother and us children (my younger brother, Vinay Verma and myself). The visits became more frequent and longer each time.

My parents had come for a visit to the Ashram for Mother's birthday darshan of February 21, 1943. Upon leaving, the Mother said something to my mother and on the return journey by train, my father asked, "What did she say?" She replied that the Mother had said, "Wind up everything in New Delhi and be here with the children by April darshan." My father said, "What will you do?" She said, "I must do what the Mother says." Since that first meeting she felt that here was an old connection and she had to be with her. The Mother said that my father should remain some time more in New Delhi. On April 11th my mother, a young woman, walked out on all the structures of family life as she had known them and with two children took the long train journey to Pondicherry. The Mother sent someone to receive us at the railway station. She was very happy to see my mother reach there in time for the April darshan. She took the three of us into her world of love and care, body and soul and mind, and there we have nestled ever since. I mean this in a very concrete sense of embracing all our lives and being into her own.

My mother once said to the Mother, "Mother, I don't want anything of the world, I only want that my children should be well educated." The Mother said, "Do you have faith in me?" She replied "Yes." The Mother said, "Then leave it to me." Later, when Mother organized the school, she was sometimes asked by outside people, "No exams? No degrees?" She would reply, "I am forming personalities, so that wherever my children go in the world, they will do well."

The Mother had set aside two houses very close to the main Ashram building and asked my mother to see which one she would find more convenient. My mother moved into one just round the corner from the Ashram. It had an open courtyard where we children could play — and our lives were created afresh by her. Our father used to come for each darshan and for vacations from the University until he, too, resigned from his post there and came permanently in 1945.

We were very young children in the Ashram in which there were about three hundred adult senior disciples. There were very few children. It was a very special world in the Ashram, a very intense atmosphere. It was solid in its density. We were aware of the great majestic presence of Sri Aurobindo there in his room and the Mother, whom we met a few times every day. The very spaces of the main Ashram building were full of the presence of great beings, the senior disciples who lived in the many rooms there. We were very conscious of these beings who were all one-pointed in their concentration and their endeavor to follow Mother and Sri Aurobindo in their work of realizing the spiritual goal before them. These presences were powerfully felt in our daily lives. We felt them even in silence, as we moved about the Ashram — it

was as though they were pouring their very being into us like
empty jars. This receiving from them is something that one
is still conscious of today. I spoke to Nirod-da, one day,
about this and he nodded and said very simply, "This was
Mother's work." As though it was part of their work for the
Mother to thus give of themselves to us. Such was the world
we lived in and grew up in as children. This was our "home"
— of concentration, with the aspirations, the effort, the goals,
the one-pointedness. Once we were there as children, the
Mother took our presence very seriously. She set about organizing life for us in the way it was possible at the time. She
put my brother and me in the charge of Sisir Kumar Mitra, a
historian from Rabindranath Tagore's university called
Shantiniketan. The mornings were spent in his rooms. It was
not very specific teaching, but he loved us very much — and
we spent mornings on a bench on the terrace under the spread-
ing branches of the Champa tree whose flowers bore the significance "Psychological Perfection". The fragrance of that
flower is still so strong for me and carries all the memories
of those years.

Each evening my parents used to spend some time with
Sri A.B. Purani in his rooms in the Ashram learning about
yoga. They took us children along and we played on the floor
of the room at the feet of Puraniji while the elders conversed.
Dilip Kumar Roy, the great bhakta [a yogi devoted to the
Divine in the heart] and great musician and singer, lived there
at the time. Once a week in the late evening hours, he would
share hours of his music with a close circle of friends in his
house. My parents were invited and of course we went along
with them. Those were unforgettable times. It was a big hall

in a spacious house and seated against the wall was the figure of Dilip-da in his flowing orange robes, with the ecstasy of a world of love and devotion visible on his face and in all the movements of his body. A harmonium was placed in front of him and a small group of disciples gathered around him and all were wrapped in the atmosphere that permeated the hall. As children we somehow crept very close to Dilip-da. We sat on the floor and as the evening grew late we put our heads down on the floor and drifted off to sleep. The love and devotion that he shared on those evenings still lives in my being in a very tangible way.

At that time Nishtha, the daughter of President Woodrow Wilson, lived in the Ashram and as a friend of my father's she offered, very simply, and with great love, to have my brother and me share long afternoons with her in her apartment so that she could tell us stories from American history. This was to improve our spoken English. Hers was a presence of great serenity with all of her being gathered up and flowing in one direction — the spiritual. In the early afternoons we used to go to her large apartment and we would find her in one of the central rooms reclining on a chaise longue. We would sit around and she would tell us stories. She told wonderful stories of the pioneering days of American life. She was very easy in the time we spent together. She would get up and walk about if she had something to do, speaking to us all the while. It was an easy and natural flow and the impression of that serene being is still strong with me.

When was a school actually formed?

Within months, more children came to the Ashram in twos
and threes. All were about the same age. By the end of the
year Mother said, "We will now start a school." We were
about twelve children, three teachers and one classroom and
had barely any books. This was December 2, 1943. Our joy
knew no bounds because it was a new adventure. She organized work for us with teachers who were disciples in the
Ashram — Sisir-da, my mother and one other person. She
guided the teachers as to how to teach — not the usual process of teaching. She organized the subjects and followed
our work in minute detail and the teachers sent a report of
the work and the children's progress daily. She said at the
time, "A teacher has to be in perfect control of himself if he
is to guide the children." More children came and more
teachers too, who joined the Ashram as disciples, and new
subjects of study were added. She followed very closely the
progress and growth of students and teachers, the inner as
well as the outer. At this time every month or two when we
went to her she would say the following words like a direct
communication and these words were, "Find your psychic
being. Be conscious." These words were like a concrete action from her. She acted on us little children with her power
of consciousness, recreating our very beings. Around this
time Mother started to visit the homes of some of the disciples. She came to our house on my 17th birthday. I remember her sitting in my mother's room and at some point I was
alone with her. She spoke about all the possibilities that life
offers, adding that my path was the one that would lead to
spiritual realizations. She always said, in so many words,

what was to be done in the future. She always spoke about the future. It was about that time that one or two really powerful experiences, which I took to Mother, gave a clear form to my inner aspiration. It seems too much to put into words and I might say I understood nothing of it at that moment and I do not know if I do now. But this aspiration took the form of wanting the Absolute — or whatever was the spiritual reality — in life and not by rejecting life, by leaving it aside. This was very clear.

The four days in the year when we had the darshan of Sri Aurobindo and the Mother, seated side by side, were of such power and presence that I would like to share how a growing young person experienced those moments. For days before each darshan the presence of Sri Aurobindo, of which we were conscious in our everyday lives, moved into a wider space and with greater intensity. It was felt all over the Ashram compound and the main Ashram building and flowed into the spaces of the streets around the Ashram. Our house was on a corner of one of those streets and one walked into this kind of presence that was solid and there was the feeling of *entering* something in a very concrete manner. This grew to its fullness on the day of the darshan itself. Sri Aurobindo was seated on a couch in the first room where he lived and the Mother was to his right; to one side was Nirod-da. In front of them was a large wooden box into which, as disciples approached them, they laid their offerings of flowers and garlands of Tulsi leaves ("Devotion"). We went up in a file standing only for a moment in front of the Divine Presence on earth and then moved on. As children we went with our parents. Soon I wanted to stand alone before Sri

Aurobindo, so I started going on my own. I was about thirteen years old at that time. Sri Aurobindo sat with the majesty of the Divine, immobile and absolute. We looked into
his eyes, into that vast, impersonal look. His eyes penetrated
so deeply that one seemed to dwell only in the Immense.
Even as a young person without understanding, without having the proper words to use, it came in very simple words
that this was *it*. Whatever the "it" meant one did not know
and who can say that it is known even now or will ever be
known. But the feeling remained that there was nothing beyond... that *this* was the Absolute. On one occasion I just
happened to be in the line behind Dilip Kumar Roy. There
he was... his being and his very body swaying in his love,
devotion and bhakti for Sri Aurobindo. Lost to the world and
only conscious of him. Peeking from behind the flowing robes
I saw the vast, impersonal look on Sri Aurobindo's face. Also,
focussed in a look of recognition, the impersonal changed to
the personal and became a point of Light. That golden face,
where never a muscle moved during darshans, creased into a
smile. This is what something in me was looking for. I wanted
to experience this more often. I would wait in the courtyard
for Dilip-da to enter the Ashram gate on darshan days, swaying in the ecstasy of the meeting to be, and as he took his
place in the file I used to slip in behind him. This way I had a
few more moments to see Sri Aurobindo. I peeped to the
right of Dilip-da in the front, to the left — no one else noticed, no one else was stepping out of the file. I could see Sri
Aurobindo so many more times and then Dilip-da stood in
front of them and I peeped to the right and could see Sri
Aurobindo with that look and that smile and feel something

of that moment between them. Untouched by time, those moments still hold their power and sweetness for me. Sometime in 1948 the Mother called me and another girl, a friend, and said to us that Sri Aurobindo has written something and we will try to dramatize it. This was the dialogue between Love and Death from *Savitri*, his epic poem, which had not as yet been published. She gave us typed sheets and gave me the role of Death and of Love to Amita Sen. I asked her, "Why have you given me this role? Death seems so big a thing." She said, "Death is nothing to be afraid of. It is a great power that has to be conquered." She called us to the long room in front of the "seat" for darshan days. She stood at one end and we were at the other. She would read out the lines and teach and show us how to do the same with power and emphasis on the words. She trained us for some time, for a few weeks, and then announced to our great and unexpected joy that Sri Aurobindo would hear us. We were absolutely thrilled and thought "we will have a fifth darshan this year"! The Mother set about doing the make-up for us. She also took out some clothes that were with her. For me, as Death, she found a black chantilly lace gown that had belonged to her Egyptian grandmother. I wore this over a grey slip. Amita was dressed in white. The make-up was Guerlain and applied by the Mother. When the great day arrived, a chair was put in the central room of the three adjoining rooms and the Lord heard us seated in that room with a wall between us, so we did not see him. It seemed somehow that they wanted to know what a dramatization of lines from *Savitri* could convey. The following year there was a presentation in the Ashram playground and over the years the dramatization of *Savitri* has become a very special regular activity of the Ashram.

This was also the time when, with the arrival of Pranab, the work of physical education was started in the school. In the early days, the Mother took a walk around the main playground and asked a few of the women present to join her in the walk and she thus formed what came to be known as "The Mother's Group" or the "Ashta sakhis" [eight companions] of Mother. Over the years they used to accompany Mother whenever she left the main Ashram building to go to the playground. She started to play croquet with them — an old French game, set up "tug-of-war" teams and she put these women, who were in their early thirties and only accustomed to wearing saris, in white shorts and shirts and a headgear called "kitty caps" for their playground activities. The younger boys and girls were organized into various groups under the overall care of Pranab with his team of group captains. A detailed and varied pattern of physical education gradually came into being as an essential element of the expanding activities of the school. The body needed to be made a conscious base for the descent of the spiritual force.

When did the Mother give you the name Aster?

It was around this time that the Mother gave me a new name. I was about eleven at the time. The name given me by my father was Mira. Mother said to me, "I have a new name for you. It is Aster, a French word." She made me pronounce it after her several times so that I got it right. She added, "Don't let anyone pronounce it in the English way!" She gave me the flower — a daisy-like flower — and told me that the spiritual significance is "Transparency". She also gave me a little bottle of perfume by that name made by Houbigant, the French perfumer. I still have the bottle. So, Aster is the name I have always used but the name Mira is very dear and very special to me as well.

Describe the atmosphere in the Ashram when Sri Aurobindo left his body in 1950.

Early one December morning in 1950, we awoke to the feeling that our entire world had drawn to a close when our father told us that Sri Aurobindo had left the body. We understood nothing but felt very deeply the gravity of the moment. He had left his body on December 5th. The day of Samadhi was fixed for 9th December and during those days we were allowed to go up to his room once each day. The older disciples were seated in specific spots in those rooms, as indicated by the Mother, and we would stand in his room by the bed, stricken and silent. But the body was *grandiose*. There was a fullness of substance and light, solid with a Presence which one felt as something of profound *magnificence*. The day of Samadhi, the Mother asked us all to put a handful of earth as the Divine Body was laid among flowers. Something came down in our being like a heavy lid and we looked up to the window on the first floor where the Mother stood. I have never been able to forget the way she looked at the time, alone in a strange and inexplicable way, stricken but without losing strength, pale but like a column of light. The twelve days that followed were intensely difficult. All the activities of the Ashram came to a full stop. All was subdued and heavy under cover of a hush. Then came the New Year and the Mother, like Durga, and with renewed energy, took up afresh life and its activities. It was in those early months of 1951 that she held a convention to which she invited educators and other leaders of the country to announce the formation of a Sri Aurobindo International Centre of Education.

She said that Sri Aurobindo was in our midst and with all the power of his creative genius was initiating this further growth of what had so far been the Ashram school. A whole program of Higher Courses was started, of a five-year duration, in subjects such as philosophy, integral psychology, math, literature. Highly qualified professors in these subjects were already there as disciples. Students just completing school years moved into these areas of higher learning with great enthusiasm. This movement of growth and expansion of reaching out to the country, which began at this time, gained in momentum right through the fifties. In 1954, Pondicherry, which had so far been part of the French regime in India, was reunited with the country at large, with the French leaving. At this time Mother addressed the President of India expressing her long cherished wish to become an Indian citizen since this was the land of her soul and of her conscious choice. She said she would like to keep her French citizenship because in her spirit the two harmonized perfectly well and that she could be of service to both equally — and universally. Leaders of all walks of life in the country visited the Ashram and sought her advice for the work they were doing. This included Pandit Nehru and Mrs. Indira Gandhi.

Would you speak of some of the work that the Mother gave you?

Well, the very first work that the Mother gave me, as a child, was to arrange flowers in large trays that were then taken up to Sri Aurobindo's room and to hers. The flower room was in the main Ashram building with three senior disciples looking after it. Mother asked me to join them and to collect flowers that were growing in the Ashram compound. Some of these flowers had a special significance given by the Mother and each flower was to be counted, even the buds. These were flowers of "Service", "Sri Aurobindo's Compassion", "Transformation", "Realization" etc. On a piece of paper, in each tray, one wrote the number of flowers and buds that were arranged there. Then they were taken up to their rooms, some to Sri Aurobindo's and others to the Mother's. This work gave a joy that still remains. When all the trays were ready, laden with flowers, one looked at them with reverence as they were being taken upstairs.

[The next phase of Aster's life in the Ashram was that of work with her father given to her by the Mother. As mentioned earlier, Dr. Indra Sen was a well-known Professor of Psychology and Philosophy at the University of Delhi.]

My father met Dr. Carl G. Jung in his university days. Dr. Jung was in India on a personal research project and he encouraged my father to go to Germany for doctoral studies. He did so and studied Hegel and Jung, lived near the birthplace of Kant and taught Sanskrit and Indian philosophy at

Dr. Indra Sen, Aster's father, at his home
in Pondicherry

the University of Koenigsburg. After receiving his doctoral degree he returned to India to continue teaching and lecturing. He presented many famous papers on psychology in academic circles, one of which was titled "The Urge for Wholeness". For him the study of psychology was not enough without a corresponding spiritual realization. He wanted a realization in consciousness of the spiritual truths of existence. After reading the works of Sri Aurobindo he found the basis for this "wholeness" approach which would make the experience a fact of personal corroboration. The only term that could be rightly used for this was "Integral Psychology". He referred this term to Sri Aurobindo, who accepted it as the proper term for presenting his psychological work.

Would you share something of the work that you did for your father?

The Mother said to me one day with great emphasis, "I want you to work with your father, to be with him in whatever he does. Your studies will come after." I was, at that time, following the five-year courses in Philosophy and Integral Psychology — the latter was given by my father in the Ashram Centre of Education. His other work at that time included receiving, at the Ashram, a number of dignitaries, leaders and other guests from outside, and attending national scientific conferences to present Sri Aurobindo's work. I shared in all this work and travelled with him. I took up all his secretarial work, typing out his writings and handling large amounts of correspondence.

Earlier, when I was about sixteen, one day Mother said, "I

want you to teach. It is nice to be with little children." I said, "But I am studying." Her reply was, "You can do both." I said, "I don't know how to teach." She said, "I will tell you." She asked me to bring the children to her — about twelve of them — each morning after classes. They were five years old. Each day I sent up a notebook with an account of what we had done. She wrote back with her comments about the children. She told me something I have never forgotten. "Give the children freedom. One is never too young to be given freedom, but the right atmosphere must be created." The meaning of these words has been like a pathway of discovery all through the years. This pattern of study and teaching always carried on for me. My students grew in age — along with me.

Somewhere in early 1955 a very rich inner period began. The presence of Sri Aurobindo was very living in the atmosphere. There was such a palpable impression in terms of consciousness, almost visual, that he was very busy doing "something". Very, very busy. One did not know what that "something" was but the feeling of his image, and of his being busy, was real. It was so strong that I spoke to the Mother about it. This seemed to always happen in the evenings when she was in the playground. When I asked her about this the first time she gave a smile of utter sweetness when I said, "Sri Aurobindo seems to be busy, what is he so busy doing?" She replied with the same sweet smile, "You will find out."

Every few months during that year I would go up to her, always in the playground, when she was there in the evenings, and I would say, "Sri Aurobindo seems to be very busy. What is it, Mother?" She would again say with the same smile, "You will know." I came to recognize this specific sweetness in Mother's smile when she spoke of Sri Aurobindo. Months passed and we had the meditation in the playground on the evening of February 29, 1956. [The day that the Mother brought down the Supramental Light into the earth's atmosphere.] The next morning, March 1st, when I went to see the Mother she asked, "Were you present at the meditation last evening? Did you feel anything?" My poor response to Mother was that I was there but had a rather heavy head! She said, "What Sri Aurobindo was busy with has happened." As the year advanced, there was a great richness of inner growth — steady growth.

After a few years another movement of the being began to take shape. The Higher Course was completed, I was teaching and the work with my father continued but something else was taking shape. I had read Sri Aurobindo's works in the Ashram but something in me felt the need to read him in the setting of the thought and culture of Europe, as though there was something for me to learn from that perspective. I spoke to the Mother about this and she asked, "Where would you like to go?" From deep within me came the response, "Paris, to the Sorbonne."

I knew nothing about the Sorbonne but the inner move was direct. Mother was happy that this was the choice and said, "It will be good for your growth to concentrate on this work."

1962 to 1970 were the years of a sojourn in Europe with Paris as base. A year after reaching there the Mother wrote me a message for my birthday that led me on another path of discovery. She wrote, "This has been a year of inner and

outer progress. May the next year continue in the same way."
The phrase "inner and outer progress" was a new one for me
coming from the Mother and made me look at this whole
process of growth in a growing perspective of wholeness.
My question was: What is outer progress in the light of the
Mother? Is it a shaping of the outer personality in harmony
with the inner being? Is this what she meant? Years followed
with intellectual enrichment and varied cultural inputs, new
ideas, new forces rushing in with always an inner base to
receive them. A re-reading of Sri Aurobindo's works in that
context was another experience. Then there began to take
place a reversal of the traditional European "rationalistic"
values. There was an urge among the youth of the time to see
life as lived, as given in experience and not only in concep-
tual terms. A larger perspective began to emerge with a great
deal of initial confusion. There was a major student uprising
at the University of Paris in 1968. I kept writing about it to
the Mother who was most interested in what was taking place.

The doctoral thesis I was working on was nearing completion. It was the first time that a work on Sri Aurobindo
had been accepted by the Sorbonne. [Aster received a Ph.D.
from the University of Paris (Sorbonne) in Comparative Philosophy. Her doctoral thesis was "A Comparative Study of
the Philosophies of Sri Aurobindo and Henri Bergson".]

On a visit home to Pondicherry during that period, I asked
the Mother, "This work is nearing completion, what should I
do next?" She said, "You will know about it soon." It was
also about this time that I felt in a very concrete and unambiguous manner that a new curve of culture, a cycle of growth
for man was beginning to discern itself on the horizon and

that horizon spanned the work of Sri Aurobindo. It appeared that this work was to take place from where he was physically centered — around Pondicherry in India.

After submitting my thesis, which was very well received with a lot of interest in Sri Aurobindo's "Supermind", I received a letter from the Mother. She said that the United Nations in New York was holding a World Youth Assembly to commemorate its 25th anniversary. This was to take place in August of 1970. A youth delegation from each country would be present, without the participation of adult representatives, at the United Nations. They would discuss contemporary issues of life with regard to education, culture, economics, politics, etc. She wanted me to be present as part of the official Indian delegation to represent the Ashram and Auroville. The Ashram I knew but I was not there at the founding of Auroville, but I was aware of Sri Aurobindo's work and such a presentation could cover both. The Assembly consisted of two thousand people drawn from all countries of the world, An eighteen-member Steering Committee was elected. The way events followed during the three weeks of the Assembly was an incredible experience of how the Mother's Force worked to shape world situations. It was so concrete in its action in all details. The consensus of the Assembly was that it was the whole personality that should be developed in the course of education and the world's interactions should take place in a spirit of unity and understanding. What a "whole" personality is was not made clear but the sense of the "whole" was there, as also a very strong sense of unity among the participants.

I was back home in Pondicherry by the end of 1970 and

after the long years away the entire being came to rest in the courtyard of the Ashram. There was a long interview with the Mother early in 1971 on my birthday — when she gave all the indications needed for the further lap of the years in this life, or in others, who knows? She said that she had already given me an indication of the work to be done. She spoke about India and said, "India is open to the deeper consciousness and the new Forces that wish to manifest. India represents the Life Divine on earth. It is this that one must manifest — in action, in life, in the manner of being." She said she had already given the direction. She added that this was the direction to follow and the goal was assured.

I resumed teaching at "Knowledge" in the Higher Course at the Ashram Centre of Education. With Sri Aurobindo's Centenary in 1972 there was a round of conferences in the country dedicated to an understanding of his work. A "Sri Aurobindo Chair of Philosophy" was set up at Benares Hindu University and there was an invitation to hold the Chair and do some work. A year's sojourn gave a powerful experience of the living force and might emanating from the Ganges River as it flowed through Varanasi.

Came 1973, and Mother withdrew from the body. The Divine Action is full of the unforeseen. All the external came to rest *within*. The pressure of the inner became more powerful and one could say more concrete. The forms changed but the work became swifter and more sweeping in the change it sought. A new kind of work in the physical, in the body began. A work so far unknown and unforeseen, the contours of which were only revealed step by step. But it seemed that the entire physical consciousness, including the conscious-

ness of the body itself, maybe even something of its substance, was beginning to be remoulded into something quite
different.

What Mother called the Auroville consciousness reached
out in its living dynamism and made itself known. I was teaching at "Knowledge" 4 hours in the morning and most of these
courses happened to be about matter! I thought I was remaining close to its core but a great surprise awaited me.

Once when I went to work at the Matrimandir in Auroville,
there was a pile of small pebbles and we had to shovel it into
chettis [shallow basins] and pass them from one person to
another in a chain. I stood there with shovel in hand on the
pile of pebbles but the consciousness would not relate to the
pebbles. It could not connect with them. It hung in mid-air
and I could not even, by deliberate effort, dig the shovel into
the pile. The experience was unforgettable. It made me see
that in my consciousness I was removed from the concrete-
ness of matter on the ground. There was a hiatus of being
and relatedness and I realized that my speaking about matter
was not authentic. I was not "grounded" in matter and the
words came through mid-air, suspended high. Something was
not quite right, to say the least, in my understanding of what
matter is. Something had to change and it did. An experience
of Auroville had begun and I found myself on a path which
took seven years to arrive at some kind of stability. That the
consciousness could station itself at many levels in the being
— from the mind as center, to the heart and further into matter itself. When based in matter, in a more or less steady
manner, without too much fluctuation, then the manner of
functioning of the mind underwent a big change and there

was another way in which things began to be perceived directly.

During this time all reading and writing were laid aside and I took up work which was not only just physical but seemed to be a working with matter itself. From *within* matter, from a poise of consciousness settled in matter. The work took the form of construction, preparation of food and designing clothes!

Then another line of work came into my orbit and that was the attempt to set up a Centre for Research in Indian Culture and a Centre of Indian Studies at the Bharat Nivas [the Pavilion of India] in Auroville. This work had resonated with me in the past but this time it was with another poise and movement of consciousness. Thus began a round of exploration and discovery of what India held in her core of experience and her many-sided richness. This exploration had two very unusual aspects to it. One was that it was undertaken in the midst of the interactive dynamism of a very diverse collective drawn from many cultures of the world. The second was to see how the living realities of that experience could respond effectively to the problems and situations of our contemporary life. It was, at the same time, an attempt at discovery or recovery and an application of it to situations that were actual.

Along the way, I felt the need to discover what was the potential of the cumulative reservoirs of energy that lay hidden in the great Himalayas. In the heart of the Kumaon region is a small center which Sri Aurobindo called "our foothold in the Himalayas". In this spot I experienced an "integrative" power of energy unlike any other that worked in matter. Awaiting me was another big surprise. This was not a remote other-worldliness of energy but where the spiritual and the material came together as one reality. This exploration continues and becomes fuller with time.

A new dynamism in an effective action on the life and being of man — uniting the spirit with its form, becoming the spirit in manifestation — seems to be almost there. Almost, but not altogether. Such a presence rides the crest of the being — more one cannot say.

The Mother's work will be done... in the eternity of Her becoming.

*   *   *

Aster's talks at the AUM 2003, the scheduled morning sessions, afternoon workshops and informal talks elicited an overwhelming response from those attending.

On Friday, May 23, she spoke informally about her days in the Ashram and how the Mother would transmit her power of Shakti through her multiple aspects and personalities. She would be all strength, all love and absolute beauty. She would gaze deeply into the inner beings of children and adults alike, moulding them and transforming the resistances to their spiritual growth. During her workshop on "The Power of Beauty", Aster said:

"The seeking for Beauty is a powerful force for doing yoga". The Mother has said, "Let beauty be your constant ideal — beauty of the soul, of the sentiments, of thought, of action, of work, so that nothing comes out of your hands that

Aster Patel at AUM Conference in
Los Angeles, Ca. May 2003

is not a pure and harmonious expression of beauty. And the
Divine's help will always be there."

Our seeking for the Divine — in the world of form —
looks for its expression through "beauty". It is within a growing perfection of the form that there lies the fulfilment of this
seeking. But to arrive at the fullness of this perfection, the
form itself needs to retrace its journey to its source in the
Spirit. It needs to get absorbed in it — with its contours of
separateness — and recover another dimension of form, which
is expressive of the Spirit in its wholeness. Then, to re-find
its place in the physical world — in this world of matter. A
matter transformed by the Spirit and a form made whole.

This matter is not only what constitutes the world around
us and outside of us, so to speak — but pertains as much to

all that makes up our human personality, which has its base in it. Even our very body, our sensations, impulses, feelings and our ideas, to a large extent, are grounded in matter. The re-shaping of all these elements by touches of the "psychic" in us is the pathway to beauty. Beauty that expresses the Eternal... in the forms of wholeness, of beings-in-matter.

All ocean lived within a wandering drop,
A time-made body housed the Illimitable,
To live this Mystery out our souls came here.

Sri Aurobindo

General Krishna Tewari

Krishna Tewari

*(Retired two-star major general in the Indian army
and in charge of the Auroville Archives)*

I first met Kamla and Krishna Tewari in Santa Cruz, California in 1990 while attending an Auroville meeting there. They were visiting from Auroville and I thought they were just about the most charming two people I had ever met. They are warm and open and highly enthusiastic; so full of wit and ideas and a sparkling youthful energy. They immediately made me feel as though we were old friends and that's the way it remains. General Tewari's presence evoked in my memory a song from one of Gilbert and Sullivan's famous light operas called "The Pirates of Penzance". The song goes: "I'm the Very Proper Model of a Modern Major General with Information Vegetal and Animal and Mineral. I know the Kings of England and Quote the Fights Historical, from Marathon to Waterloo in Order Categorical." Krishna's dignified and disciplined military bearing and his handle-bar mustache just made me think of that song and I could not stop singing it in my mind each time I saw him during that visit to Santa Cruz!

Krishna joined the Indian army after his graduation in 1941. His two army awards consisted of the Param Vishisht Seva Medal and the Ati Vishisht Seva Medal. During World War II he was twice mentioned in despatches by the British for his services in Burma and Malaya.

His wife, Dr. Kamla Tewari, joined the army after he was captured by the Chinese in the 1962 war to be able to support the education of their three children. At that time the Government of India had not yet finalized the scheme for payments to the wives of prisoners of war and widows of those killed in action. Kamla's father was Major General A. N. Sharma, who was the retired Director of Medical Services of the Indian Army. Her eldest brother, Major Som Nath Sharma, won the highest gallantry award of free India in 1947 posthumously during Pakistan's attack on Kashmir. Another brother, Lieutenant General S. N. Sharma retired as the Engineer in Chief of the Indian Army and the youngest brother retired as the Chief of the Army Staff. It was quite a distinguished army family indeed! Their two families were long known to each other and Krishna knew Kamla when she was studying medicine in the Lady Hardinge Medical College in New Delhi. They got married soon after her graduation and both retired from army service in 1976 after which they moved to Pondicherry with their family.

The following are some questions that I put to Krishna and his answers:

Where were you born?

I was born in Jullundur City in Punjab on October 2, 1922.

What was your family life like? Were your parents spiritual or religious people?

We were a very well-knit family with seven children. My

father was the Medical Officer of Health in the city. He was a strict disciplinarian and set a fine personal example for us children. He had a devotion to duty and a strong sense of responsibility. My mother was deaf from childhood, but had mastered lip reading. She was the life of the family while our father was of a more serious nature. She was a scholar in Hindi and never had a shortage of stories to tell us from our ancient scriptures and other tales. One could say that we were a religious, God-fearing family and there was a special prayer room in all the houses in which we lived. Our grandfather and my father's widowed sister lived with us and her children were also brought up with us. We had regular kirtan and bhajans [Hindu religious services and songs]. My sister, who was the eldest among us and my elder brother and I studied under private tutors at home until I went to a public school at the age of fifteen.

What were your special talents or childhood ambitions and dreams?

I was a sickly child and received some special attention from my elders, but the discipline of my father was imposed on all of us equally. Perhaps I was also a bit too sensitive by nature, but I was very considerate of others and did not invoke any jealousy among the other brothers and sisters even though my elder brother was a bit of a bully.

Were you aware of a spiritual presence in your childhood? When did you first begin to recognize and aspire for the spiritual life?

I am not conscious of any special spiritual presence in my childhood but, as I have said, we were brought up in a deeply religious atmosphere. I do not know when I started aspiring for a spiritual life. Maybe it was during World War II in Burma when I saw death and senseless destruction and experienced a number of narrow escapes personally. That obviously set me thinking of Divine protection when so many of my friends were dying in battle. There is a Hindi couplet which says "One who enjoys Divine protection, cannot be killed by anyone."

> *How do you see your early life as being influential to coming to this yoga?*

One heard the word "yoga" from early childhood but there was no attempt at any practice of it, except for regular prayers, until I moved to the Ashram on retirement from the Army at the end of 1976.

> *When did you learn of Mother and Sri Aurobindo and when did you come to the Ashram to live? Can you describe your darshans with the Mother?*

I was introduced to the Mother (and Sri Aurobindo) in 1971 while I was posted in Calcutta. We were preparing for the war with Pakistan that resulted in East Pakistan becoming an independent country — Bangladesh. I have given a comprehensive account of this in the book I have written under the title "A Soldier's Voyage of Self Discovery" in two chapters under the titles "War for the Liberation of Bangla Desh" and "Divine Intervention in 1971".

It happened while the crisis was building up before the actual war and after I had been told of the top secret plans. I was deeply involved in the preparation for war with limited resources at my disposal. One morning in my office, I must have been in a reflective mood in the light of the immensity of these impending operational challenges, when one of my officers, a Lieutenant Colonel who worked in the same head-quarters, came to me and asked with a smile, "Sir, why are you so pensive these days, which is so unlike you?" I told him in a friendly tone, "Chum, you would be more pensive if you had some of the problems I am facing these days which I cannot share with you at present." He had come prepared (I had no idea that he was a long-time devotee of Sri Aurobindo and the Mother) and he promptly said, " Sir, you are my old instructor and I should not be advising you, but I have a humble submission; whatever your problems, write to the Mother for her blessings." I hesitated for a couple of days. I had heard of Sri Aurobindo but knew little about the Mother in Pondicherry. Then I wrote a few lines just to seek her blessings for some problems I was facing in my work which I could not specify. I received her blessings in a few days and the rest is history. Most of the top brass at the East-ern Army HQ had received the Mother's blessings prompted by the same source. It is amazing how successful the opera-tion against Pakistan was when over 93,000 regular Paki-stani army soldiers surrendered to the Indian Army.

From my point of view, it was clearly a Divine Interven-tion. The Mother had shown a great deal of interest in the developing situation in West Bengal. So, as soon as I could,

I travelled to Pondicherry with my family. On February 22, 1972 we were granted a very powerful and special audience by the Mother. One by one we sat at her feet and gazed into her eyes as we were told to do. Not a word was uttered as each one of us received her blessings. She looked deeply into our eyes pouring her Force into us. She put her hand on our heads and gave each of us a rose and a blessing packet.

This meeting is what brought about the major change that was to take place in my life. Independently all the members of my family — my wife and our three daughters and I — decided to settle in Pondicherry in the Ashram and we moved there permanently in November 1976 after my retirement from the Army.

The biggest regret in my life has been that I never went to Pondicherry to see Sri Aurobindo during the intensive training we did in South India. It was 1943 before we were sent to war in Burma. We were involved in exercises within close proximity to Pondicherry but I never even thought of going there to receive Sri Aurobindo's darshan. Perhaps I was just too involved in the preparation for war.

> *Can you describe the Ashram atmosphere since the Mother left her body? How has your sadhana changed since Mother left her body? What new forms, if any, has your sadhana taken at this stage?*

I met the Mother only twice, once described above on 22nd February 1972 and a second time later that year. Both times not a word was spoken but her powerful presence was so deeply registered in my mind that I can still feel that pres-

General Tewari receiving AVSM award from the
President of India 1972

General Tewari receiving PVSM award 1977
(with wife Dr. Kamla Tewari)

ence any time it is invoked in all sincerity. This has happened many times in my life.

That beautiful formula given by the Mother, "Remember
and Offer", can be applied to any facet of life's activities to
one's advantage. One misses her physical presence but it
hardly makes any difference to the Sadhana. If one's faith
is unshakable, there is little difference. This is so even
though I met her only twice in my life, for brief periods. No
words were exchanged. There was only her physical presence.

[Krishna had told me earlier that he had been advised to
put any questions to the Mother that he liked but he was so
overwhelmed during his time spent in her Presence and so
overcome with psychic emotions that he could not speak.]

> *What changes do you see taking place in the Ashram in
> the future and will it be different from what it is now?
> In the same manner, what do you foresee for Auroville's
> future? Will the two institutions work more closely
> together in the future?*

I am not in a position to talk about what changes I can see in
the near future in the Ashram. In her physical absence, I
expect there are problems faced by those entrusted with the
task of running the Ashram. In Auroville there are numerous challenges and problems as well. There are problems
connected with the international status and development of
the city for a capacity of 50,000 inhabitants (at present there
are only about 1700 people from over thirty-two countries).

There are also challenges of all kinds such as no hierarchy, no rules and regulations, acquisition of land from individual holdings and speculators' activities, relationship with the local population, financial constraints, developmental approaches. There are also the kind of difficulties Auroville went through late in the 1970s and early in the 1980s, which resulted in intervention by the Government of India — just to name a few.

Aurovilians have to go through deep introspection in the light of the four-point Charter of Auroville given by the Mother in order to truly move forward. One has to constantly remind oneself that Auroville will be built by invisible forces as she had hinted and remind oneself that the Mother acts quietly, unseen, if one's personal ego and ambitions are kept in check.

The very concept of the Auroville project is a challenge and difficulties come constantly to prove the validity of the Mother's statement, "Difficulties are opportunities for growth"— each difficulty is a step in which to move forward if faced with the right attitude.

It is my belief that Auroville is poised for a breakthrough but the present 1700-odd Aurovilians (which includes children) as well as those likely to join in the future, have to be true to the ideals and work consciously for a true human unity.

Would you give advice to new spiritual aspirants that would help in their development and help them to integrate their lives in the world with its focus on materialism and the vital life, or is each better off seeking his or her own way?

The only advice one can share is to work for a true surrender and control of one's ego, for devotion and full faith in the success of Sri Aurobindo's and the Mother's vision. This should be done, whatever the odds, and one must consciously observe these ideals particularly in the midst of day- to-day life in the external world with all its challenges.

Is there a disadvantage in never having seen Mother and Sri Aurobindo in their physical bodies?

It is certainly my deepest regret that I never had darshan of Sri Aurobindo in 1943 while we were training for war and moving around in South India. I consider it very fortunate that I had darshan of the Mother with my family. That was certainly the most unforgettable moment for each one of us. I may add that the Grace we have all received since then has been a definite advantage to us.

Now that you are eighty-one years old, what has yoga done for you at this stage in your life?

I must correct you. I am not "old". You could say "almost eighty-one years young". I had previously led a very active and adventurous life. I believe this unique yoga sadhana of Sri Aurobindo and the Mother has kept me young with a capacity, energy, will power and confidence to carry on actively the work in their Auroville which has been called a "living laboratory" by her. We are the so-called "guinea pigs" on whom experiments are being made by the Divine.

> *One difficulty always occurring in sadhana is straying from the path, doing what one knows not to do and becoming discouraged. Did this happen in your own sadhana? How is one to guard against this and what to do if and when it does?*

One does get shaken when difficulties and disappointments come in life but I have always kept alive in my mind the assurance by the Mother that difficulties are opportunities for one's growth. There is little doubt in my mind that when one has truly surrendered to them these so-called difficulties are deliberately created by the powers that be with the intention of helping us to move forward and make progress.

> *Could you share any special stories or anecdotes that you remember of the Mother and any advice she gave you for your sadhana?*

After my first meeting with her on February 22, 1972 and after our return to Calcutta, I had decided to seek a premature retirement from the Army and move to Pondicherry to be close to her. Worth mentioning is the fact that this decision of wanting to move to Pondicherry at the earliest was spontaneously taken by all of us in the family independently.

I had informed one of the Mother's secretaries by telephone of my decision to seek premature retirement. I was called by telephone in Calcutta a couple of days later with a categori-

cal disapproval by the Mother of my intention. In fact I am
told that four times she said, " He is not to leave the Army.
He must continue in service. He must not leave the Army.
We shall decide when he is to leave." I had to withdraw my
application even at the cost of being laughed at by my bosses.
I had no idea at the time that I would receive my promotion
to the General's rank so soon after and be decorated as well
with the second highest service awards of PVSM and AVSM.

After retirement in 1976, I had to stay in Pondicherry for
a couple of years before moving to Auroville where I had set
up a farm on thirty-five acres of barren Auroville land. There
a well was bored and a house was built. In addition to the
farm, I quite spontaneously became involved in the problems Auroville was facing. These problems called for the Government of India's intervention through an Act of Parliament
to be followed by legal battles. When the Act was challenged
the case was taken up by a five judge Constitution Bench of
the Supreme Court based on the petition signed by me on
behalf of Aurovilians. In 1982 the decision came through in
Auroville's favor with an Act of Parliament called the
Auroville Foundation Act.

*   *   *

Krishna and Kamla continue actively in their work for
Auroville along with their family. Krishna is in charge of
the Auroville Archives and can be seen in the Bharat Nivas
offices of the Archives on a daily basis.

Kamla helped to organize an Auroville Health Centre in
the early 1990s (previously there was nothing of this caliber

in Auroville) and she continues her practice of medicine there.

Krishna and Kamla have four daughters. Uma, the eldest, who retired as a Lt. Colonel from the Army Medical Corps two years ago, is now working in the Auroville Health Centre. She and her doctor husband have not joined Auroville as yet. He is working in the Pondicherry Institute of Medical Sciences and they have two sons who are studying in the Sri Aurobindo International Centre of Education.

Deepti, their second daughter, is married to Arjun Puri. She is involved in education and writes the Matrimandir Journal and Arjun works at the Matrimandir. Abha, their third daughter, runs an Auroville unit called Shraddhanjali that manufactures handmade stationery and pressed flower art objects. Her husband, Claude Arpi, is in charge of the Tibetan Pavilion. Their youngest daughter, Shubha, is married to Narayanan Menon. They both hold Ph.D. degrees in physics and teach at Amhurst University in Massachusetts. They have two children.

On my last day in Pondicherry, January 4, 2003, before returning to the United States, Uma and General Tewari paid me a visit at the Seaside Guest House. They drove in from Auroville and Krishna had been very ill with a persistent fever. He was still weak and not fully recovered, but they drove all the way in to Pondicherry to see me. It was such a lovely visit. We sat and talked and of course the conversation turned towards the Mother and his darshan with her. His eyes filled with tears (those same tears of psychic emotion) and I took his hands in mine and we sat silently in one of those precious moments when two souls are simultaneously turned in adoration towards the Divine.

Amrit (Howard) Iriyama

Amrit (Howard) Iriyama

(Matrimandir Gardens and Nursery)

Amrit has been my close friend since 1969 when I lived in
Auroville. At that time we worked together at the
Matrimandir Gardens Nursery. His manner is calm, gentle,
balanced and quiet. He is a Japanese-American man of slight
but strong build, who speaks softly and who always seeks
harmony in all his actions and interpersonal relationships.
He has rarely been seen to waver from this calm inner repose, in spite of the many vicissitudes and upheavals in
Auroville, many of which have impacted him on a very personal level.

I conducted the interview in the community of "Certitude"
in Auroville at his charming and very elegantly decorated
home surrounded by cool plants and ponds filled with water
lilies. The inside furnishings are antique, mostly French-
Tamil, accompanied by tasteful and gracefully placed Hindu
statuary and paintings. The roof of the house is sloped, in the
Japanese style with a slight red trim. We sipped tea and reminisced about our days together in Auroville, as he shared
with me the following:

Amrit was born Howard Shoji Iriyama, in an American
Relocation Camp in Arizona on October 3, 1943 during World
War II. All the Japanese residents, around 110,000 individuals living mainly in the U.S. West Coast area, whether American citizens or not, were interned in such camps by the U.S.

Government during the war, and many of the American citizens of Japanese origin today were born in these camps, which were located in the desert and other inaccessible areas. They remained in the Gila Bend Relocation Camp, on a former Indian Reservation, for two years, then were relocated to Colorado, where the family established a farm before eventually returning to California.

> *How did being born in the relocation camp impact your philosophy of life and your spiritual development?*

It made me question social conditions, how individuals are treated, and nurtured dissatisfaction within me toward the social order as it existed. Later, after discovering Sri Aurobindo, I read what he had said about the generation of souls born during World War II, that many had come into the world to counter the dark influences of that era. This generation born in the early to mid 1940s had a lot to do with the peace and civil rights movements in America. All of this came to maturity in the 1960s, when Auroville was also founded. Because of the War and my childhood experiences, I had a very strong aspiration towards human rights and a greater sense of equality for all of humanity, an ideal to which I felt deeply connected. Because of this, my favorite writer of the American Revolution was Thomas Paine, a man who suffered much for his idealism, and I had a tremendous sympathy for the many revolutions at the time against despotic rule and tyranny, for example the Hungarian and Czech revolutions against Soviet rule. I remember weeping when the Hungarian revolution was crushed so mercilessly. I was only thirteen years old at the time.

What was the religious life of your family?

My family was Buddhist, my grandfather Zen (meditation and knowledge) and the others Jodo Shinshu, the Pure Land sect (devotional). After being allowed to return home from our "relocated" place in Colorado, we lived in Guadalupe, California, then moved to Santa Maria when I was six years old. Since there was no Buddhist temple in Santa Maria, I was sent to a Methodist Christian church attended mostly by other Japanese. As a result, I became a devoted Christian, regarded Christ as my ideal, and at twelve years of age chose to be baptized, something that took my mother by surprise. She asked me, "Why did you do that?" I answered, "What do you expect when you send me to a Christian church?" You see, Buddhists are not so strict about such things.

My family had an extensive vegetable farm in the Guadalupe-Santa Maria area, my grandfather having been one of the founders of the California truck farming industry in the early 1900s. Farming was the main economic support for the Japanese community in America before the War and to a lesser extent also after. After the War there was a kind of Diaspora throughout the continental U.S., as before the War the Japanese were concentrated mainly along the West Coast and Hawaii.

I remember at the age of three, returning home to California from Colorado. Much like the migrants in Steinbeck's *Grapes of Wrath*, I stumbled out of a big truck filled with our family belongings clutching a red metal toy airplane. In the

toy plane, a fly had somehow become trapped and died trying to escape. This remained indelibly imprinted in my mind
as the existing condition for all human beings. Another feeling that would suddenly come upon me was, why was "I"
born in *this* body and not in that of another? It seemed strange.
And I often felt that by being born, I had fallen on my head
and did not really belong here.

In my childhood there was still a lot of prejudice against
the Japanese. I could hear my parents talking to others about
the camps and the situation of the Japanese in America, but
they never spoke to us children about it. Sometimes other
children would chase me and throw stones. I simply could
not comprehend why some people would suddenly stand and
stare at me. Then I understood, as I grew older, why doors
were shut in my face, that the slant of your eyes and the color
of your skin actually made a difference to some people!

As a child I learned to play the piano moderately well and
came to have a deep love for classical music. Academically I
did very well and graduated first in my class in high school,
as well as achieving second place in the field of liberal arts
in the Southern California State competitions in 1961. I attended Stanford University, majoring in Japanese language
and literature, and won the Freshman Achievement Award
for being in the first percentile of my class. Then after three
years of hard work, I was elected to Phi Beta Kappa, the
national honor fraternity reserved for the academic elite of
America.

In the summer of 1964, under the sponsorship of SNCC
(Students' Non-Violent Coordinating Committee), I decided
to go to Greenwood, Mississippi, to teach history and Eng-

lish in one of the Freedom Schools set up at that time for the black community there and to register voters. It was an intense period, during which there were some killings and much threat of violence. I remember the sheriff of Greenwood blocking off both ends of the street where the SNCC office was located, setting up a machine gun on top of one of the cars, and shouting hysterically, "I ain't responsible for what happens!! I ain't!!" Luckily I am still here to talk about it. Later on, a film was produced called "Mississippi Burning" which dealt with that "summer of '64" and the murder of the three civil rights workers in Mississippi. However, I experienced some disillusionment with regard to this kind of social action. I came to realize that such problems could not altogether be rectified through external social action. This led me to search further for the truth. I knew there must be another way, one of which I was not yet aware.

Though I was still interested in Christianity, after having gone through a period of agnosticism, and contemplated entering a Christian seminary and monastery, I was slowly drawn to Zen Buddhism through the person of Suzuki Roshi, a Zen master in San Francisco. For the first time, I had come into contact with someone who was truly different, who lived what he taught and appeared to manifest what I was looking for. I wondered at his wisdom, simplicity and childlike spontaneity. So under his inspiration I decided to become a Zen monk. I was to enter his main monastery, Eiheiji, in Japan and then return to help him in his work in the San Francisco Zen Center. At that time talks were also going on about starting a monastery in California, Tahsuldara, which was later to become the largest Buddhist monastery in North America.

In August of 1965 I went to Japan and studied Japanese language at the Tokyo Stanford Center, International Christian University, under a Rockefeller scholarship, which was renewable for two more years up to my doctorate. During my time in Tokyo, I stayed at the extension temple of Eiheiji and regularly spent the weekends in Yokohama where I attended "sesshin" or intensive meditation sessions. There I was given a "koan" or puzzle to which there is no logical answer. The first koan, for example, is, "What is the nature of a dog?" the answer being "Moo" or the Japanese word meaning "Nothingness", negation. I was simply asked to concentrate on this syllable, "Moo". During an intensive "sesshin" lasting one week, the concentration became so heavy that I began to have severe pains in the chest. To ease the pressure, the teacher gave another exercise, which was simply to keep my attention on a samurai or warrior standing in front of me, holding a raised sword, which would immediately kill me if I took my gaze off it.

Strangely enough, this resulted in my first decisive spiritual opening. Suddenly my body became stone-still, the breath seemingly non-existent, and it appeared as if "I" were in a silent room looking out through the windows of my eyes at a world passing by like the scenes on a cinema screen. Thoughts entered like silver blips from a vast silence, and I realized that the mind had fallen silent, and that we do not "think", thoughts only appear from a kind of universal silence or mind field. Sleep became luminous, it was like being enfolded in a cocoon of light, and I became aware of others' thoughts and feelings. It was like floating in a silent light, joy and ecstasy, with judgments and perceptions that seemed immediate and true. I could even play badminton better, more infallibly! The breath appeared to enter as light through the forehead, and I could see concretely all the organs operating in the body. And in this silence, I found myself communicating with a feminine being who emanated wisdom about life and death, a being I later in India came to identify as "Kali". The detachment and peace, lack of desire, was total. Later I came to understand that the answer to the first koan given to me, i.e. "Moo", was in fact the silent mind.

How did you come to discover Mother and Sri Aurobindo?

I came into contact with the Mother in March 1967. I was still in Tokyo in the summer of 1966 and decided to enter the head monastery of the Rinzai Zen Buddhist sect, Shofukuji, in Kobe, the head Roshi being Yamada Mumon, where I stayed for several months.

After my intense inner opening, there was a corresponding fall in consciousness, "as high, as low", so to speak. As my experience slowly began to recede, only then did I realize something had happened. It was like a fish in water. While in the water, it is so natural that it is not even conscious of it. Out of the water, it struggles and begins to die. I felt like this, I began to suffocate, as if I were dying, the life force slowly draining out of the body, with a very strong pressure for the consciousness to go up and out through the top of the head leaving the body. The ordinary life and consciousness had become as death for me. Nonetheless, some effects of this opening have still remained with me to this day. It was then that the Mother and Sri Aurobindo came into my life.

Tim Rees, an Englishman also interested in Zen, had been in Tokyo studying for his doctorate in Geological Engineering, but later left for India. After his arrival in India, Tim sent me a letter saying that I should meet his Master, Maharishi Mahesh Yogi, whom he had discovered. By this time I was so ill that I felt my choice was either to die in Japan or go to India. I decided to go to India. In the meantime, Suzuki Roshi met me in Tokyo and scolded me, "You are wandering, you are lost and sick, you will die in India." I answered, "I don't know why, but I feel compelled to go, I *have* to go." He only responded quietly, "If you have to go, then go." I felt as if I had jumped off a cliff, in total freefall, leaving everything familiar behind, all security, anything I could hold on to, in the hope that someone or something would catch me and save me from being dashed on the rocks below. So I left Yokohama by ship for India in October, 1966, a journey that took one month, throughout which I remained terribly ill. On November 5, 1966, I arrived in Bombay. I met Tim in Delhi, from where we travelled together to the Ashram in Rishikesh.

[At this point Amrit told me that when he was a child of twelve years old, a Force would come into his body during sleep, very material and dense, and would often be accompanied by a milk-white light, very pure and dynamic. As soon as he arrived in India, the penetration of this force through the top of the head became stronger and stronger. After coming into contact with the Mother, he recognized it as her Force and Light which had been with him since childhood.]

After four or five months in the Ashram in Rishikesh I quickly realized that this guru was not the person I was looking for. Paul Horn, the American flutist, was also there at the same time, just one year before the Beatles. Mahesh Yogi could not explain this force that continued to descend into myself, and I was feeling increasingly uncomfortable with him. Then in March of 1967, Tim again introduced me to someone else, one Sandeep Mukherjee, a devotee of the Mother and Sri Aurobindo. Mukherjee confirmed this descending force as that of Sri Aurobindo and the Mother and as a mark of their yoga, instructing me to meditate on the Mother's image surrounded by a blue light. Immediately upon doing this, I felt an inner release, as if I had come home after a long journey. From that point my health began to improve and the feeling of leaving the body disappeared.

Besides Sri Aurobindo and the Mother, Mukherjee had another teacher, whom he called Baba Sharadanand, with Ashrams in Cooch Behar (West Bengal) and Okhimath in the Himalayas. At the time it was rumored that this Baba was none other than Subhas Chandra Bose who founded the Indian National Army to help free India from the British. According to the story, though Bose was supposed to have died in a plane crash, he survived, had a spiritual turning to the yoga of Sri Aurobindo and the Mother, and was now the Baba Sharadanand of Okhimath. There were many reports in the newspapers that this Baba was indeed Bose, and apparently Mrs. Gandhi herself even attempted to meet him. Strangely enough, it was this Baba who sent Mukherjee to Rishikesh, telling him he would meet some foreigners there, and that he was to instruct them in the yoga of Sri

Aurobindo and the Mother! And indeed, he did meet some of us and did give instructions about concentrating on the Mother.

In the summer of 1967, we met Baba Sharadanand near Haridwar. He spoke very educated, clear English, and bore a striking resemblance to Subhas Bose, with his high forehead and very powerful personality. From the questions he asked each of us, it was clear he understood our weaknesses. Baba asked me, "If you have a choice between everything the world has to give and a life of suffering for the Divine, which would you choose?" I answered, "A life of suffering." He said rather pointedly, "Do you have the guts for that?" I answered, "I don't know until I try!" Then he laughed and said, "All right, all right." I don't like much pain and suffering. This whole story of Baba and Subhas Bose has always remained a mystery to me, though it is clear that it is through Baba that I came to Sri Aurobindo and the Mother.

From the beginning of my contact with the Mother, I began to correspond with her through Pavitra, a Frenchman whom the Mother was later to describe as a yogi of extraordinary spiritual accomplishments. In mid-1968, I wrote to the Mother saying, "I feel your love and your presence, but I do not know who you are." Then on July 18, 1968, in a state of semi-sleep, I felt the pressure of the force and myself falling into a very deep well. As I fell deeper and deeper, I became frightened and began to call out to the Mother. Suddenly I heard a voice saying, "Yes, one day you will know who I am. You will have in life a power of action...." She said other things which I could not remember as the mind became active. The voice was exactly the same as that of the Mother which I later heard on tapes. Though I could not immediately understand the meaning of what she said, later I understood.

After a stay of a couple of months at Ramgarh in the Himalayas, in October 1968 we all went to visit the Sri Aurobindo Ashram in Pondicherry — Mukherjee, Tim Rees, an Englishwoman (who later died), a Japanese Buddhist priest named Horizawa, John Mandeen, who later became an Ashramite, and myself. We were a motley group of people dressed like mendicants! It was then that I visited Auroville for the first time.

When I first came into contact with him in 1967, Mukherjee had told me some things about the unusual date 4-5-67 about which both Sri Aurobindo and the Mother had spoken previously. Mukherjee mentioned that on 4-5-67 things would be decided and that there might be a general destruction. During that period, he disappeared, apparently to be with Baba, and when he returned, I asked him about this date. He said, "The will of the Universe has changed and things have been partially decided."

In December 1969, in Auroville, I first met Narad [Richard Eggenberger], who had asked Nolini, the secretary to the Mother and someone recognized in the Ashram as a yogi of great spiritual attainment, about this date. Surprisingly he answered in almost exactly the same words, "It has been partially decided." Then as Narad started to leave, Nolini called him back and explained further, "In the past, a complete pralaya [destruction] has been necessary. This is why the Mother wants Auroville. Auroville will contain the essence of this present civilization."

Coincidental?

Another instance in 1968, Mukherjee told me, "The Mother is withdrawing and wants people to find her inside." The following was the Mother's message on the dining room chalkboard on the day of my arrival in the Ashram in September 1969, "I am reducing the physical contact with the disciples, because I want them to find me inside."

At the end of 1968 I received a Quit Notice from the Government of India, that my visa was being cancelled and I would have to leave India. I wrote to the Mother explaining the situation and asking if the Ashram could provide a guarantee. Through Pavitra, she answered that as I am not an Ashramite, the Ashram could not provide such a guarantee. But she added an assurance, "Have trust that in the end, everything will work out for the good of your soul and the fulfilment of your spiritual destiny." Then she closed with her blessings. I proceeded to the Sri Aurobindo Ashram in Delhi where I explained the problem to Mr. Jauhar, the man responsible for the Ashram there. He told me not to worry and arranged for someone to take me to the head of the Visa Department in the Home Ministry. It seems this man had once been an Ashramite in Pondicherry! I got the visa.

After this, I became a personal assistant to Mr. Jauhar, helping him with correspondence. He wanted me to stay on in New Delhi in this capacity. However, after having received the Mother's permission for a birthday darshan, I left Delhi and returned to the Ashram in Pondicherry in September 1969. After my arrival in Pondicherry, Mr. Jauhar sent me a telegram saying he hoped I would make the right decision and return to Delhi.

Just at this time there were also problems with the American Government in regard to the Vietnam War. As I was totally opposed to the War, I had sought C.O. status [Conscientious Objector], objecting to serving in the military on grounds of religious conscience. As I told the military board I wished to become a Buddhist monk, they exempted me from military service on grounds of being a priest. However, after realizing I had come to India, the board decided to reclassify me as being eligible for military service. I had even gone to the US Consulate in Madras asking what would happen if I renounced my US citizenship. Quite upset, the Consul told me I would be immediately thrown in jail as soon as I set foot on American soil!

When I wrote to the Mother about this problem, her answer was simply, "Be quiet." Oddly enough, it was in 1970 when I was supposed to report for the military draft back to America, that the then President Nixon suspended all draft calls and introduced a new system, the lottery system, to determine who should report for the draft. A year later I received a letter from my local draft board that the order for me to return to America had been withdrawn, and I would not have to report for military service because my lottery number was too high. And it seems that an order had been sent for me to return, but I had not received it. It had been lost. Grace in action!

Would you describe that birthday darshan with the Mother?

Frankly, I could not really connect physically with the Mother. The connection was always inward, and I communicated indirectly through her secretaries. I feel the Mother did not feel it was necessary for me to have so much of an external relationship with her. She wanted me to find her inside. This was always the message I received. This birthday darshan was quick, only a minute or so, but led to a series of events that were to determine my future for many years to come. What followed after that first darshan was clear. I had approached Nolini many times asking him to put before the Mother my request to join the Ashram. Each time he would reassure me that he would definitely speak with the Mother about this. Shortly after this birthday darshan, I was invited by a friend to visit Auroville. We cycled out to Auroville and went to the community called "Hope". After this, I returned to Nolini and again asked him if he had asked the Mother if I could join the Ashram. He simply sat there silently for some minutes without speaking, then suddenly said, "Mother does not want more people in the Ashram unless they have some specific talent or work they can do. What can you do?" This, in spite of his constant assurance that he would present my request to the Mother. Then it was I who was at a loss for words. I stood there totally speechless and nervous. "OK", he laughed, "What are you interested in?" As a reflex action, I blurted out, since I had just come from there, "Auroville", even though I had no real interest in it. He immediately replied, "Go to meet Navajata." Navajata was the Chairman of Sri Aurobindo Society which was sponsoring Auroville. I met Navajata who said he would ask the Mother about me. In a few days, he returned with word that the Mother had accepted me into Auroville. On October 10, 1969, I officially joined Auroville. Over the following year I struggled against this decision and wrote several letters to the Mother requesting her if I could leave Auroville and join the Ashram. In my last letter, I wrote, "You said the Ashram was for those who wish to dedicate their lives to the Divine. I wish to do so, and want to be in the Ashram, not Auroville. But if you think it is best for me to stay in Auroville, I will do so. But I say very clearly from my side, that I do not wish to be here." The answer from her secretary, Maggie, very clear and unambiguous, was, "It is better for him to remain there in Auroville. He can do what he wants there (dedicate his life), *I know it*." I stopped asking.

In December 1969 I met Richard Eggenberger, later to be given the name "Narad" by the Mother, on the Auroville bus. He told me that the Mother had given him the work of designing all the gardens that were to surround the Matrimandir. He asked if I wished to work with him, and soon obtained the Mother's permission for this. At that time I was living in "Hope". The Mother soon asked through Nata, an Italian man who founded the Auroshikha incense factory, to see all of us individually from the "Hope" community. When the Mother saw my photo, Nata said she expressed a great deal of interest, though he thought it was because I represented the Japanese people. During the darshan, for about ten-fifteen minutes I was alone with the Mother as she gazed into my eyes. As an aspiration began to awaken in the heart, she broke into a beautiful smile.

After that darshan, an odd thing happened. In early January 1970 I felt a very strong force pushing me towards the center of Auroville. As I started cycling towards the center, I felt as if something were physically driving me in that direction. I began to walk around in the vicinity of the Matrimandir, when I came to a spot shaded by a few mango trees. Immediately I knew this was to be the Matrimandir Nursery. I contacted Narad and we went to the center together. We walked around and came to the same place. Though I had not mentioned anything about this to him, Narad immediately turned to me and said, "This is going to be the Matrimandir Nursery!" And so it happened.

We began by planting Portulaca [the flower that Mother calls "Sri Aurobindo's Compassion"] at the Amphitheatre for the Mother's 21st February birthday in 1970. In the beginning the workers were, of course, you [Anie], Narad, Jean Finney, Danielle, a Tamil boy named Ramachandra and myself. The conditions in those days were quite primitive. Food was a problem. We grew a vegetable garden and took turns cooking meals for each other. There was no toilet, no electricity and no running water. Water had to be brought in twice a day by bullock cart in containers. The only vegetation in the area was a few mango trees. We made wooden benches and flats and planted flower seeds, and the white ants [termites] were so severe that our baskets were in shreds by morning. The first flowers planted were Marigolds, named "Plasticity" by the Mother. I still have that first flower sent to her. She also named many Hibiscus, for example, "The Beauty of Auroville", later called "The Beauty of the New Creation". These were times of great struggle, with the cows and goats destroying in a minute what took months of work, with the

Amrit at age 8 in California

Amrit, Narad, Ramachandra and Anie at the invocation of
Matrimandir February 28, 1970

elements, the torrential rains and blinding dust storms, the incomprehension of the villagers, and most of all with the weaknesses of our own natures.

Some new and important developments began for me in early 1972. I began a study of astrology, along with a number of other Aurovilians, with Patrizia Norelli-Bachelet, author of *The Magical Carousel* and other books on astrology and numerology. After discovering how to apply Patrizia's conception of the nine-year Gnostic cycle to the personal horoscope, using Sri Aurobindo's "Siddhi Day", 24 November 1926 (actually there are three dates connected with the triangle of fire), as the beginning of the Aquarian Age (as intimated to me by a friend, also a former student of Patrizia's), I continued to build on this and realized that this was the "reversal of the horoscope", an ancient knowledge revealing untold spiritual possibilities of astrological wisdom. Using the sign of Capricorn as the key, I discovered how to place the astrological signs on the earth, and how, as these cycles sweep over the earth, certain energies and events are activated, both upon the earth and in the personal horoscope as well. In fact the more the awareness and consciousness of the individual evolve and develop, the more there is a resonance with these universal movements in what one may term the cosmic horoscope. All of this has led to a greater understanding of Sri Aurobindo's yoga, and how the energies released affect the evolution of the earth, as well as one's personal evolution through inner openings and experiences. This knowledge continued to grow, like a structure developing brick by brick, until at the end a finished building is in place. I also came to understand that knowledge is not the prerogative of any individual, any more than a pipe through which water flows can claim ownership over the water. It is only the channel. All life is like this.

In August 1972 I left the Matrimandir Gardens Nursery and Auroville, and went to live in the Ashram in Pondicherry. On January 1, 1973 I returned to Auroville and lived in the house of William Netter [a New York designer] at "Certitude". It was there that Shyama [a Swedish woman, mother of Auroson] and myself started a rose garden with Mother's permission and blessings, receiving a card on which she wrote in large letters, "ROSES, BLESSINGS", a card which I felt ultimately was meant for the Matrimandir Gardens. On her 95th birthday, her last, we planted 95 "Surrender" roses. On November 17 that year the Mother left her body. Following this there was a severe drought, and most of the roses died. It was so symbolic.

I remember sitting at the Ashram Samadhi under Mother's room the evening before she left, as I had been staying with a friend in the Ashram. Early in the morning on the 18th November 1973, someone came to our room to inform us that the Mother had left her body, and that we should hurry to the main Ashram building. This reminded me of my dream experience of 1969. At that time many people in the New Delhi Ashram were saying that Mother was ill and would leave her body. That fear was in the air. In the dream, I saw people very agitated, running about saying, "Mother has left the body." Then in the dream I saw her standing on the Samadhi clad in a beautiful flowing white sari, and she said to me, "You know, in the end we can do nothing for ourselves, we live in eternity." Then she gave this wonderfully radiant smile. It was like a dam breaking, and I was flooded with adoration towards her. I understood then what true devotion and surrender were, very powerful and uncompromising. In this way she indicated what our attitude should be if and when she would leave her body.

In the days that followed, I used to go every day to the Ashram, to meditate at the Samadhi. During that time I experienced a rainbow of Force from the Samadhi pouring into Auroville for days and days, so strong that I felt physically as if I were flying back into Auroville, effortlessly.

In 1974 I began to work on the Matrimandir construction, then in the outer gardens digging pits and planting trees. This was a time of hard physical labor, which went on until about 1977. November 4, 1975 marked the beginning of serious troubles for Auroville. At that time Shyama came to me and asked for my signature as a witness on a document legally forming the "New Auroville Society" in contradistinction to the Sri Aurobindo Society, Auroville's parent body. This was to give us more say over our internal affairs. I signed, not realizing what a bombshell it was. In the beginning very few Aurovilians supported this movement. However, miscalculations and heavy-handedness by the SAS began to alienate residents more and more and gradually forced increasing numbers into joining the movement. Around Christmas of 1975, I was called into Navajata's office for a visa interview. The interview has been published in *Sun Word Rising*, a book about Auroville written by Savitra a.k.a. Alan Lithman. Navajata told me that I would have to "collaborate" with the SAS or I would have to leave Auroville. My visa was in fact the first to be threatened. These methods only aggravated the situation. Under pressure, I became increasingly hostile and bitter.

It was at this time, however, that a dream came to me, giving me an inner indication that I had to change my direction. In the dream, there was a hostile force circling around my house. I decided to attack it and drive it away. When I opened the door to do so, it immediately entered the house, and I found myself outside, the hostile force inside, laughing, mocking at me saying, "You see what you have done!" I understood. By attacking frontally the darkness, I opened myself to it and allowed it to enter. Then there is no longer any difference between oneself and the darkness one is fighting. I realized the only solution was to stay quiet and not open the door, and battle the darkness inside. Even then, it took many years to work out what had already entered.

After this, John Walker, an American living in Auroville, gave me a Sri Chakra, a Tantric yantra [geometrical object used in ritual worship] related to the worship of the Supreme Mother, the Shakti in India. Just holding it I experienced waves of ananda or bliss emanating from it. I wondered how a geometrical figure could give such a spiritual experience. Exactly then an unpublished conversation was given to me in which the Mother speaks of the fifth aspect of the Mother, the Mother of Ananda which she wrote is also the Mother of Transformation. I also found through reading that the Shakti of the Sri Chakra is termed the Anandamayi or the Mother of Ananda. That my experience was directly connected with the meaning of the Sri Chakra further stimulated my curiosity. With this connection between the Sri Chakra and the yoga of Sri Aurobindo in mind, I approached Madhav Pandit, a scholar in the Ashram known for his writings on the Tantra. His immediate advice was to meet Panditji, a Tantric yogi in Rameshwaram who had often met the Mother, and whom Mother had recommended to many sadhaks for help in certain areas of difficulty. He told me Panditji could help me understand the Sri Chakra. Then Madhav Pandit told me of his own experience. He said that one day the Mother called him and told him to meet Panditji in Rameshwaram. He mentioned that even though he was not interested in any other guru, he followed Mother's advice and proceeded to Rameshwaram to see Panditji. Madhav Pandit then added, "Mother prepared the ground, Panditji gave the opening." With Madhav Pandit's recommendation letter in hand, I went by train to Rameshwaram.

On July 18, 1977 I found myself on the doorstep of Panditji's house, the words "Sri Aurobindo Nilayam" carved in bold letters over the entrance. Immediately on seeing me, Panditji began to laugh and said, "So, you have come", as if he had been expecting me! He asked, "What do you want?" I answered that I wanted to learn about Sri Chakra. Then he said, "If you want to know, you have to do the practice. There is no other way. I will give you the first mantra, and after three months I will give you full initiation and you can begin the puja." Six years of intensive sadhana followed, involving up to eight hours a day of puja, japa, meditation and preparation, until 1983 when I returned to America for my first visit after eighteen years. This was followed by about six more years of less intensive practice. These twelve years were the most difficult, yet at the same time the most fruitful in terms of inner experience.

Tantra is basically a fusion of the three aspects of Joy (ananda or love), Knowledge and Power, i.e. the power and joy of effectuating knowledge in the creation, which is the Divine Mother. The aspect of knowledge has always been important to me — the thirst to arrive at an understanding of what everything is aiming at. The one thing that was always very clear from the beginning was that an inner guidance and grace were continually present, protecting and showing me the path to greater spiritual growth. This I attribute to the Mother. And I feel that the inner growth of these years provided the basis for what was to come in later years, particularly regarding the work at the Matrimandir. I met Panditji exactly nine years to the day after the experience in which the Mother said I would know who she is and would realize a "power of action". This of course refers to Tantra.

How and when did you receive the name "Amrit"?

In 1970 I had written to the Mother about receiving a new name. She said, "Howard is all right for the present," indicating that I would receive a new name in the future. During my work with Panditji, he gave me the name "Amrita-nandanath", meaning "Lord of Immortal Bliss", or simply "Ambrosia" or "Nectar".

Would you please speak of your years of work at the Matrimandir?

I worked for a short time with the construction team on the Matrimandir. I could not get accustomed to the heights, especially after Diane's fall. [Diane was a young Belgian woman who fell from the scaffolding of the Matrimandir in 1976, resulting in paralysis.] Diane was on the scaffolding trying to climb up, when she grabbed a loose pipe, lost control and fell around 75 feet to the bottom of the Matrimandir excavation. I could hear her hitting the bars as she fell. The bars broke her fall, bending in the process, but saved her from dying. After that, for some months, I helped take care of her, massaging her, trying to bring life back to her limbs. I just could not go back to the construction job. People were in shock as they felt something like this just could not happen. Diane died in 1985. Diane had already suffered a deep shock when her five-year-old child, Auro-Louis (also the son of Guido, another Belgian national), fell into a well in Kottakarai and drowned a few years before her fall. Auro-Louis had been given his name by the Mother. He was a very sweet child, but he looked to me like a little soul who had fallen on his head at birth, appeared dazed and did not know who or where he was. I could identify with Auro-Louis, because as a child I felt very much the same way.

In 1974 we worked in the Matrimandir outer gardens, digging pits, mixing compost and planting trees. We would start at 7 or 8 a.m. and work until sunset. It was back-breaking work, but it was a grace to work so hard to create something beautiful. I had never been physically oriented in such a way, but the work was satisfying and fulfilling. This went on for over two years.

The fighting between the SAS and the Auroville community intensified, and peaked between 1980 and 1982. In 1980 the Government of India promulgated the Auroville Ordi-

nance temporarily taking over the administration and assets
of Auroville from the SAS, which resulted in a court case in
the Indian Supreme Court, ultimately settled in Auroville's
favor. In 1988 this resulted in the Auroville Foundation Act
which formalized the Government intervention in Auroville,
at the same time according Auroville some protection for its
ideals. The result of this conflict for me was a period of isolation from the community. I concentrated solely on my
sadhana. Externally times were terrible and very painful, but
inwardly very rich. In a sense it was a real grace. I was ostra-
cized because of the path that my sadhana had taken me on
and because I had chosen not to take sides and to become a
"neutral" in terms of my political position. This isolation was
in fact a very real protection, because it prevented me from
participating in acts I could never have lived with later. And
it enabled me to concentrate on the only thing important, my
inner sadhana. During this time I received very clear inner
guidance. Around any major event that occurred, dreams
would come indicating what the outcome would be and what
direction I should take.

On October 3, 1988, on my birthday, it was announced
that, apparently according to a Government directive, there
would be "no more factions or groups" in Auroville. I, along
with a number of others, was formally accepted back into
the Auroville community. From that time I began working
once more in the Matrimandir Nursery and Gardens, and in
January of 1990 became a part of the group management of
the Nursery [Narad had left Auroville by this time]. By the
latter part of 1990 I had become the main person responsible
for work at the Nursery and soon became a member of the

general management of the Matrimandir, the MMCG [Matrimandir Management and Coordinating Group]. So the situation had reversed from total exclusion to a position of total responsibility.

In 1995, because of difficulties in the visitors' organization, I was asked to help reorganize the visiting procedure. In the process, we studied the Mother's statements about access to the Matrimandir and attempted to implement them in as practical a manner as possible. This took a few years to formulate and establish as an effective procedure in all its details. This involved the visiting procedures, passes both for visiting and meditation, Matrimandir Chamber duties, reception of VIPs, access for residents and general Auroville access. I was still responsible for the Rose Garden that had begun in 1991. It has now grown into a beautiful garden with many varieties of "country" roses, inspired by the blessings given by the Mother many years before.

Then in the middle of 2001 I took responsibility for the reorganization of the general Matrimandir security. After establishing some basic changes and norms, from the end of 2002, I have withdrawn again from everything except the Nursery. I felt the need to return to my roots, the place where I had begun in Auroville and to concentrate on my sadhana. It seemed that I had become too externalized, and too many controversies were going on that were not helpful to inner progress.

Summing it up, this whole life has been an exposure to different religious orientations and spiritual paths. I was born into Buddhism, baptized into Christianity, initiated in Hindu Tantra, instructed in Sufism, and guided through all these experiences by the Supreme Shakti we call the Mother. What I have learned from all these paths is that each approach leads to a particular inner experience, and that each experience contributes to a more total, complex and rich spiritual realization which can be a more solid basis for Sri Aurobindo's yoga of transformation. In short, all these spiritual paths have helped me to understand Sri Aurobindo's yoga in greater depth. Buddhism leads to the silent mind, Christianity to devotion, Islamic Sufism to the science of the heart and Hindu Tantra to the effective manifestation of the Divine's Will upon the earth, i.e. the Shakti.

In a symbolic manner, these disciplines also encompass all the levels necessary for a total spiritual attainment as described by the Mother: the physical or religious level which lends itself to expressions of devotion through certain movements of the body; the vital corresponding to the level of occultism; the mental to that of spiritual philosophy and understanding; and the ultimate level of pure spiritual experience.

From the time she withdrew from her body, it has been clear to me that for Auroville, and perhaps for the earth also, the Matrimandir is the receptacle holding the Mother's Force. This Force, on an external level, seems to produce chaos at times, but this is a process of her work of transformation that will ultimately lead Auroville to its goal. This is at least my faith, that this process will lead to the fulfillment of Auroville's true purpose.

Finally, I would like to say I have come to the following conclusion, that for myself and I think for all those in Auroville, to concentrate on bringing forth the soul within, with its accompanying light, joy and sweetness is the only hope and the most important work to be done. And I can say that over the last few years, this state of inner happiness and joy has been growing and remains for me the only base for stability in an increasingly chaotic world. For this is the touch of the Supreme Mother, the grace and guidance that uphold us through all the vicissitudes of life.

Matrimandir Auroville 2002

The Auroville Rose Garden – Jan. 2004

All that thou hast, shall be for others' bliss,
All that thou art, shall to my hands belong.
I will pour delight from thee as from a jar,
I will whirl thee as my chariot through the ways,
I will use thee as my sword and as my lyre,
I will play on thee my minstrelsies of thought.
And when thou art vibrant with all ecstasy,
And when thou liv'st one spirit with all things,
Then will I spare thee not my living fires,
But make thee a channel for my timeless force.
My hidden presence led thee unknowing on
From thy beginning in earth's voiceless bosom
Through life and pain and time and will and death,
Through outer shocks and inner silences
Along the mystic roads of Space and Time
To the experience which all Nature hides.
Who hunts and seizes me, my captive grows:
This shalt thou henceforth learn from thy heart-beats.
For ever love, O beautiful slave of God!

SRI AUROBINDO
(*Savitri*, CWSA Vol. 34, pp. 701-702)